A FULL-L

Get Smart

adapted by CHRISTOPHER SERGEL

from the Series originally created by

MEL BROOKS and BUCK HENRY

and produced by Talent Associates, Ltd.

THE DRAMATIC PUBLISHING COMPANY

*** NOTICE ***

GET SMART

A Comedy in Two Acts

For Ten Men and Seventeen Women

CHARACTERS

MAXWELL SMART.... *secret agent for CONTROL*

HELEN
MYRA
JANE } ....*students*
FRED

PROFESSOR DANTE...................*a scientist*
PROFESSOR ZALINKA...............*his assistant*
AGENT 44....................*a CONTROL agent*
CHIEF....................... *head of CONTROL*
MISS FINCH.......................*his secretary*
HODGKINS.........................*his assistant*

MAN
WOMAN } ....*at bus station*

GARTH
MARY WONG
SHIRLEY WONG } .... *KAOS agents*
BETSY WONG

MR. BIG ....*head of KAOS*

BIG SISTER
LITTLE SISTER } .... *travelers*

AGENT 99.....................*Smart's assistant*
AGENT 13 .... *another CONTROL agent*

ANN
JILL
MAY } .... *four blondes*
LAURA

PRINCESS INGRID ....*also a blonde*

PLACE: *Washington, D.C.*

TIME: *The present.*

ACT ONE

AS THE HOUSE LIGHTS DIM OUT: Light comes
up in front of the curtain. Two students, HELEN
and MYRA, come on in front of the curtain R,
wheeling in a small table on which is an odd little
mechanism. *[Any unidentifiable bit of apparatus
will serve.]* The two girls are being extremely
careful. Meanwhile, a VOICE is heard, either
through a public address system, or spoken by
an actor standing offstage.)

VOICE (low key, official-sounding, serious yet confidential). Attention. Your attention, please.
This is Washington, D. C. Somewhere in this
city is the central office of an organization known
simply as CONTROL. Its exact location is top
secret. Its business is counter-espionage. (The
two girls are positioning the table.)
MYRA (to HELEN, hushed). *Very* careful.
HELEN (hushed, in reply). I *am* very.

(Meanwhile two other students, JANE and FRED,
are coming on in front of the curtain L, where
they pull on a stand with curtains around the
base.)

VOICE (continuing). And somewhere on the campus
of an important university near Washington, a
scientist is about to test a tiny scale model of a
new instrument known as the "Inthermo"--an in-

strument so powerful it may alter the present structure of world power. Such a device, of course, would be a prime target for KAOS--the international organization of evil.

JANE (hushed). Fred--what about the target?

FRED (also hushed). Target?

JANE. For Professor Dante's test.

FRED (going back off L). Oh--sure--I'll get it.

VOICE (without pause). Happily for the free world, the evil forces of KAOS are countered by CONTROL. (With greater intensity and more confidential.) Right at this moment the bright torch of liberty is shielded by one of CONTROL's top employees--a man who lives a life of danger and intrigue--a man carefully trained in every art of a secret agent.

(MAXWELL SMART is coming on R, in front of the curtain, during this. He is wearing a hat and trench coat. His movements and mannerisms clearly proclaim his profession.)

VOICE. This man has expert professional knowledge of every deadly weapon. He's adept at Karate and Jiujitsu. He speaks many languages. Above all, he's a master of disguise--able to assume a protective coloration for whatever terrain he encounters. (As this is said SMART takes off his hat and trench coat, revealing himself dressed in a wildly out-of-date "Joe College" outfit. The VOICE continues without pause.) In other words, he can melt into any background--go unnoticed as a part of any group. (Both HELEN and MYRA do a "take" on Smart's appearance.)

MYRA (incredulous). You've got to be kidding.

HELEN. Who *are* you?

SMART (speaking deliberately). Maxwell Smart--a

fellow student--here to assist Professor Dante with his experiment. (He tosses coat and hat off R.) Excuse me.

(FRED is coming back on L, carrying an "object" --any sort of container which can hold some concealed flash bulbs.)

FRED. He's using a tough target for the experiment. (Looking in container as he sets it on stand.) They're globes of hardened steel.
JANE (calling R). Where's Professor Dante?

(MYRA gestures R, where PROFESSOR DANTE, a preoccupied man wearing a lab smock, is coming on in front of the curtain.)

SMART. Hi there, Prof.
DANTE (with distaste). Prof? (To HELEN.) Where's Professor Zalinka--she's to assist.
HELEN. She stopped to make a phone call.
SMART (suspiciously). Phone call?
DANTE (patiently). Professor Zalinka is absolutely dedicated to the success of the Inthermo.
SMART. I see.
DANTE. All of you--over here. (FRED and JANE come R, while HELEN and MYRA take positions above and to the right of the table holding the "Inthermo.")
FRED (as he crosses). The targets are like armor plate.
DANTE. Exactly.
JANE. Won't the Inthermo injure the building?
DANTE (shaking his head, happily). No, no--just the target.
SMART. Maybe you better explain how it works-- simply.

DANTE (indicating mechanism). This tiny scale model is about to demonstrate how the basic principle of reactive thermal concentricity holds true. Actually, the dynamics of the catalytic phenomenon is expressed in direct ratio to its initial molecular conclusion.

(PROFESSOR ZALINKA, an attractive but severe-looking woman wearing a lab smock and carrying a clipboard, comes on R.)

SMART. Right. (Pause.) Maybe you better explain it even more simply.

DANTE. You try, Professor Zalinka.

ZALINKA (slowly so SMART can follow). If Farmer Brown takes five molecules to the market--and Farmer Green takes *three*----

SMART (interrupting). Okay--let's get on with the test.

DANTE (inspecting mechanism). I have it programmed for the little cylinders of hardened steel on that table--we make a minor adjustment--keep back out of line, all of you--R-e-a-d-y---- (DANTE apparently activates something on the bit of apparatus, and as he does so, the concealed flashbulbs in the container on the stand are touched off. There is a general gasp.)

MYRA. Wow!

HELEN. It worked!

FRED (awed as he peers at stand). They've been incinerated!

JANE. By the little scale model.

DANTE (sadly). This is terrible.

MYRA. Terrible, Professor Dante?

DANTE. I was almost hoping it would *not* work.

ZALINKA. But why?

DANTE. This is just a miniature. Think of the destructive power of a full-size Inthermo! Think of such a weapon in the wrong hands! (They all stare front with wide-eyed horror at this thought.)

VOICE. Yes, think of it! Think of such a weapon in the hands of KAOS. (Pause.) No, no--it's *un*thinkable. (At this everyone relaxes.) The world does not have to contemplate a potential catastrophe of such magnitude because of CONTROL-- the organization of good. (A telephone bell begins ringing and everyone begins turning toward SMART, who winces slightly at the sound, edging nervously away from the others. The VOICE continues:) Ever vigilant, the skilled secret agent from CONTROL is on guard--unnoticed-- unsuspected----(SMART is even more embarrassed at the continued ringing, especially since the stares of the others pinpoint him more and more as the source of these sounds.)

DANTE (with a shrug at this bell nonsense; he's back to business). Let's get the model back to the lab safe.

ZALINKA. Yes--I'll see to it. (They are going off R, taking the table and model with them while SMART continues to retreat L.)

HELEN (under her breath as she is going, indicating SMART). What is with that guy?

JANE (also under her breath). That ringing sounds like--but it couldn't be.

ZALINKA (sharply). Careful, you----(Controlling herself.) Take it easy, students. (As they all go off, SMART leans back against the stand at L and snatches off his shoe. He holds it like a telephone. The ringing stops.)

SMART (into shoe--as though into a telephone). Agent 86, Maxwell Smart, here.

CHIEF (over P.A. or by actor playing the role from behind the curtain). 86--report to headquarters immediately.

SMART. Wait a minute. Who is this?

CHIEF. This is the Chief. Who else would be calling you on your shoe?

SMART. Well--there's no such thing as being *too*
careful. Would you mind giving me today's pass-
word.

CHIEF. This is an emergency, 86. There's no
time for----

SMART. I'm afraid you'll have to further identify
yourself.

CHIEF (angry). I'm telling you, 86, this is the
Chief. Now----

SMART. If you can't give me the password--then
I'll accept the counter-sign or today's secret
code number. My life can depend on it.

CHIEF (furiously). Get in here, Max, or I'll per-
sonally tear you apart.

SMART. That's good enough for me, Chief. I'm
on my way. (SMART slips on his shoe, starts
to leave, then stops as he remembers something.
He steps back and raps on top of the stand which
held the targets. He calls in a hushed voice:)
44? Agent 44?

(The curtains around the base of the stand are pulled
aside, and the face of a young man emerges--a
face on which nervousness and indignation fight
for control.)

44. You *knew* I was here, 86, but you didn't stop
them from going ahead with the test.

SMART (incredulous). Stop them?

44. Suppose Professor Dante had aimed the Inthermo too low?

SMART. We're all expendable, 44. (Considers an
instant, then amends.) That is--*most* of us are

expendable.

44 (desperately sorry for himself). Actually--I'm
not having a very good time on this job. I mean
--no mingling with glamorous co-eds--no com-
paring notes with that Professor Zalinka--no
sports at all--no crazy student activities----

SMART. Take it easy, 44.

44 (starting to cry). I don't even get to wear a
trench coat.

SMART. Listen, what I have to tell you----

44. A spy can only take so much. Sneaking around
these corridors. Sleeping on a zinc table in the
laboratory with nothing to keep me warm but a
Bunsen burner. Hiding--always hiding---- 86, I
want to come in from the cold.

SMART. Get a grip on yourself. (Holds handkerchief to 44's nose.) Here--blow.

44 (after blowing). You won't tell them about this
back at headquarters?

SMART. Of course not. I know what you're going
through.

44 (coming out from under table and standing up).
They wouldn't like it.

SMART. Sometimes it helps to have a good cry.

44. Try telling that to the Chief. He hates to have
his men cry.

SMART (with a start). The Chief! Listen, 44--
I'm called back to headquarters. (Rushing R.)
You'll have to take over here.

44 (to himself, grimly). Another night on the zinc
table in the lab----

(SMART has gone off R, re-entering immediately,
putting on his trench coat and hat. The curtain
begins to rise.)

SMART (calling across). Guard the Inthermo with

your life.

44 (calling back). I slipped a note in the pocket of
your coat. It's important.

SMART (taking paper from the pocket of his trench
coat). Secret information?

44 (shaking his head as he pulls stand off L). Requisition for a rubber mattress. (44 completes
exit L, as SMART looks after him with distaste
for 44's lack of dedication. Then he begins but-
toning up his coat and arranging the angle of his
hat.)

SCENE: The curtain has risen now, revealing a
stage that is divided into two playing areas--
the division indicated by a low rail or wall ex-
tending from upstage to downstage for several
feet. The area U L C is the central office of
CONTROL. There is a well-equipped desk which
contains, among other things, an inter-com and
two telephones, one of which is red. There are
also some file cases, several chairs, and a large
hanging map of the world with markers stuck in
various spots.)

AT RISE OF CURTAIN: The CHIEF is sitting behind the desk, leafing rapidly through some papers. He is a fatherly type in his mid-fifties.
He is usually warm, frank and friendly, smokes
a pipe and wears a cardigan sweater under his
jacket. In times of stress, of course, he can be
grim and demanding. An attractive secretary,
MISS FINCH, is standing in front of the desk.)

CHIEF. What do you make of this, Miss Finch?
MISS FINCH. My security rating doesn't go high
enough. I haven't seen those papers.

CHIEF (with slight sigh). I've been meaning to see
   to that. While I'm talking with 86, see if you
   can find out any more about the plans of our
   V.I.P. from Scandinavia.

MISS FINCH. Yes, Chief. (She starts D R C toward
   SMART, who has just finished getting himself in
   order.)

CHIEF (after her). And don't forget to order the
   new filter for my tropical fish tank.

MISS FINCH (approaching SMART). You're expected, 86.

SMART. Call me Max.

MISS FINCH (archly). Wouldn't that be too familiar?
   I mean--an ordinary secretary and CONTROL's
   top agent?

SMART (calling back to her as he continues into office, agreeing). I guess you're right. (MISS
   FINCH goes out D L.)

CHIEF. About time, 86. (Considering a paper on
   his desk.) I thought I told you to be careful with
   Professor Dante--to keep out of his way while
   you're guarding him.

SMART. Chief--it's not my fault. The man just
   hates to be watched. He's got a thing about secret agents.

CHIEF (holding up paper). We have another com-
   plaint from him.

SMART. What is it this time?

CHIEF. He says that you've set his work back six
   months.

SMART. *Me!* Set his work back six months?
   That's ridiculous. (Pause.) Three months.
   Maybe four on the outside.

CHIEF. Max--Dante is involved in tremendously
   important work. We mustn't let *anything* upset
   him.

SMART. O.K. --let's lay our cards on the table,

Chief. Give it to me straight. Do you want to
put another man in charge of the case?

CHIEF. Max--that's not a bad----

SMART. Of course not. I know you've got confidence in me.

CHIEF. Actually--another agent on the job might
be----

SMART. So let's say no more about it.

CHIEF (with a sigh). Who's with Dante now?

SMART. Agent 44. (Pulling out paper.) He gave
me a requisition for a----

CHIEF (shortly). We'll send him a box of tissue.
I wish he wouldn't cry so much. (Looking off
grimly.) I hate having my men cry!

SMART. As long as *I'm* in charge of the case,
Chief, you don't have to worry about----

CHIEF. Not so fast, Max. I want to sort this out.
There's a puzzling new case and maybe we
should----(He is interrupted by a bell. SMART
leaps back and draws his revolver--ready for
anything.)

SMART. What's that?

CHIEF (rising casually). A reminder. (Taking
small box and starting L.) It's time to feed my
tropical fish. (As he goes off.) I've just added
some neon tetras.

SMART (calling after him). How can you take time
for tropical fish when so many important----

CHIEF (calling back from off L). Looking after
these rare fish is my only relaxation. It helps
me to think.

SMART. What's the puzzling new case?

CHIEF (off L). A kidnaping.

SMART. Who do you want me to kidnap, Chief?

(CHIEF is coming back on L.)

CHIEF. No, Max. If anything, I want you to pre-
    vent a kidnaping. (Looks back L, pleased.) My
    fish certainly like this new food.
SMART. Let's stick to business, Chief. You need
    your best man guarding Professor Dante. Once
    KAOS finds out about the Inthermo----
CHIEF. Yes, but research takes forever. 44 can
    handle a routine security job. Meanwhile there's
    an immediate problem.
SMART. What, Chief?
CHIEF. These blondes!
SMART (startled). *Blondes!*
CHIEF. In the last four days, three blondes have
    been abducted in Washington from this area.
    (Points to spot on map.) What do you make of
    that?
SMART. It's either a conspiracy or a guy with a
    very weird hobby.
CHIEF (showing SMART some photographs in which
    he is instantly engrossed). These are the girls.
    All of them were registered at the Hotel Cramley.
    86, are you listening?
SMART. Yes, Chief.
CHIEF. At first we thought it was just a police mat-
    ter, but then we began to find lots of clues point-
    ing to KAOS--almost as though they were chal-
    lenging us.
SMART (continuing to study photographs). Hmmm.
CHIEF. I couldn't see any point to it, but my secre-
    tary, Miss Finch, happened to mention something
    that has me worried. She mentioned that Princess
    Ingrid of Scandinavia is arriving in Washington to-
    day. And--*she's* a blonde, too. Any questions so
    far?
SMART (reaching for the photographs). Could I see
    number three again?
CHIEF (irritably putting pictures away). The Princess

is traveling incognito because she wants to avoid
newspapermen and security agents. But we've
got to protect her.

SMART.   I don't see why KAOS would suddenly start
kidnaping blondes--even Princess Ingrid.

CHIEF.   I didn't either, but----

SMART.   And it's a lot more important what happens to----

CHIEF (going right on).   But Miss Finch called my
attention to the NATO meeting that's about to
take place in Scandinavia. If anything were to
happen to Princess Ingrid, it could seriously
compromise our government's position.

SMART.   The three blondes being kidnaped--and
Princess Ingrid's being a blonde--and the NATO
meeting--that could all be a coincidence, Chief.

CHIEF.   I know--and there's something fishy about
it somewhere. But we can't just ignore----

(MISS FINCH is coming back in D L.)

SMART (cutting in).   We can't ignore what Professor Dante is----

CHIEF (shortly).   I'm well aware, 86, and I've no
intention of taking any chances with----

MISS FINCH.   May I come in, Chief?

CHIEF.   If it's important.

MISS FINCH.   I wouldn't know, Chief, but I found
out where Princess Ingrid will be staying--the
Hotel Cramley.

CHIEF.   I don't see what difference----(Does a
"take." Sharply.) The Hotel Cramley!

MISS FINCH.   She took a suite.

CHIEF.   But that's--the other kidnapings--this set-
tles it. I've made my decision, 86. You're to
drop everything else and guard Princess Ingrid.

SMART (protesting).   Chief--44 can't protect the
Inthermo all by himself. And once KAOS dis-

covers that it's no longer in the experimental
stage----

CHIEF. Wait a minute, Max. You said--no longer
in the experimental stage.

SMART. That's right. The Professor incinerated
some globes of hardened steel this afternoon.

CHIEF (incredulous). But it's nowhere near com-
pletion!

SMART. You mean the *full-size* Inthermo. What
he used today was a miniature scale model.

CHIEF (hushed). And the miniature incinerated
steel?

SMART (nodding). If KAOS got their hands on an
operational scale model, it wouldn't take them
long to----

CHIEF. You don't have to spell it out, Max. (Worried.) The trouble is, we're so desperately
understaffed.

MISS FINCH. Chief, if you don't mind my mention-
ing--there were some special reasons for putting
86 onto the new case.

CHIEF. But this is no time to reduce the guard on
the Inthermo. (Wishfully.) Maybe it's just a coincidence about those blondes. (The telephone
begins ringing.)

MISS FINCH. My guess is that KAOS is up to something around the Hotel Cramley.

CHIEF (picking up white telephone, into which he
speaks). Yes? *What?* (Listens, then covers
mouthpiece and speaks to others.) A fourth
blonde has just been kidnaped.

MISS FINCH (hushed). Ask where it happened.

CHIEF (into telephone). Where did--I see. Hodgkins,
if we've any new equipment for 86, let's have it.
(Hangs up and turns to MISS FINCH.) You made
a good guess--the fourth blonde was kidnaped
across the street from the Hotel Cramley.

SMART. Couldn't be *four* coincidences.

MISS FINCH (diffidently). The reason for putting 86 on the new case is in his folder.

CHIEF (flipping through a pile of folders on his desk). Let's see--Smart, Smart . . . Salzberg. Saxton, Schwartz . . . (Studies Schwartz's record.) Hmm . . . this Schwartz is a real go-getter.

SMART. Hold it, Chief, I can handle *both* cases! Think how I handled two assignments the last time. (CHIEF considers this for a moment and then picks up the telephone.)

CHIEF (into telephone). Hodgkins, send in Schwartz. Schwartz is in Rangoon? What's he doing there? Oh--he's being held prisoner. Well--as long as he's on the job. (CHIEF hangs up telephone, picks up pipe as he considers SMART again. He shakes his head and knocks the ashes from his pipe into ash tray on his desk.)

SMART. Wait, Chief. I'll have 44 at the lab, and between us, I *know* I can swing it. Chief--I'm raring to go! (SMART slams his fist down on the desk to accentuate his enthusiasm, sending the ash tray and its contents flying into the air.)

CHIEF. Max!

SMART (brushing him off). Sorry.

MISS FINCH (extracting folder from among others). Perhaps this will have the information you wanted.

CHIEF (accepting folder). Very efficient, Miss Finch.

SMART (still cleaning off the mess). Could happen to anybody.

CHIEF (reading record). Smart--here we are. Oh, yes, that's why we wanted you on the Princess Ingrid case.

SMART. The name's familiar

CHIEF (from folder). Five years ago when the Princess' father spoke at the United Nations, you saved his life.

SMART. It's coming back to me. Of course I can't keep track of everyone whose life I save.

CHIEF. The Princess was with her father at the time, so probably she'll remember you.

SMART (entirely confident). Probably.

CHIEF. That's the point--she'd know and trust you.

MISS FINCH. From what I hear--if you don't mind, Chief--it's 86 or no one. She *hates* being guarded.

CHIEF. Max, I'm putting her safety in your hands.

SMART. You won't regret this, Chief. She'll be as safe as--as the Inthermo.

CHIEF. About the Inthermo---- (Turns to MISS FINCH.) Tell Hodgkins we're waiting for that equipment.

MISS FINCH (going D L C). Right away. (She goes out D L.)

CHIEF (dropping his voice). About the Inthermo-- I'm assigning another agent.

SMART. *Chief!*

CHIEF. To assist you.

SMART (after a pause, hurt). You think I *need* assistance.

CHIEF (dead serious). Max--I'm thinking of all that's involved here. If I could, I'd put *more* agents on it.

SMART (concerned). There's something about these cases you're not telling me?

CHIEF. Call it a hunch--that's all. I've a hunch KAOS is mounting some sort of major effort. If they are, *you'll* be our front line. You could be exposed to every kind of danger imaginable.

SMART. And *loving* it!

CHIEF (soberly). There was a teletype this morning that Mr. Big dropped out of sight in Hong Kong ten days ago.

SMART (impressed). Mr. Big!

CHIEF. If he's risked coming to Washington to direct a KAOS operation----(Dismissing this with a smile.)

But I don't suppose it's *that* serious.

SMART (pause). Chief, if *you'd* feel better with
my taking on an assistant, I'll go along with it.

CHIEF. Agent 99 will meet you at the bus station
across the street from the Hotel Cramley.

SMART. How will I know 99?

CHIEF. 99 will find you and use the following
phrase: "New York Mets win double-header."

SMART (chuckling as he writes this down). Very
good. New York Mets win double-header.

(HODGKINS is coming on D L, carrying a small
case, and turns to come into the office.)

CHIEF (can't get over it; shaking his head). A miniature Inthermo incinerating steel! How does it
work?

SMART. Basically it's a conversion of heat waves
into----

CHIEF. In simpler terms, Max.

SMART. If Farmer Brown takes five molecules to
the market--and Farmer Green takes *three*----

CHIEF (stopping him). That gives me the general
idea. (Turns.) Hodgkins, I hope we've come up
with some useful new equipment.

HODGKINS (setting down case on desk and opening
it). A few surprises for KAOS this time, Chief.

SMART. All I really want is my locker key.

HODGKINS (with a faint sigh, handing over key).
Let's not stop with a locker key.

CHIEF. He's on a very serious mission, Hodgkins.
Two missions.

HODGKINS. In that case you better take this fountain pen. (Demonstrating.) Actually it's a secret pellet carrier. The smaller pellet--this one
--is a concussion pellet. When thrown against
something or activated by heat, it will blow a ten-

by-fifteen foot room to smithereens.

CHIEF (taking it from HODGKINS). This larger
pellet--it's----(HODGKINS nods gravely.) Max,
I guess you know what this one's for?

SMART. Larger rooms?

CHIEF (putting hand on Smart's shoulder). KAOS
has ways of making a man talk. If you *are* cap-
tured and if it looks *really* tough, this is your
one ace in the hole. This pill when swallowed
will bring painless death in about twenty seconds.
Any questions?

SMART. Yes--how do I get them to take it? (The
CHIEF and HODGKINS exchange a look.)

CHIEF. Let's get on to the rest of the equipment.

HODGKINS (taking silver cuff links from box). Mirror cuff links.

SMART. Can I see some in gold?

HODGKINS (irked at Smart's attitude). Really,
Chief!

CHIEF. These are serious threats, Max, and I'd
like to think we've put our trust in the right man.

SMART. No question about that, Chief. (Concerned
at the lack of response.) Is there?

CHIEF (ignoring Smart's question, to HODGKINS).
Get on with it.

HODGKINS (holding up cigarette lighter). Here's
our most exciting development--the new 27F cigarette lighter.

SMART (ignoring HODGKINS). I *am* your best man,
Chief. I'll prove it! I'll prove it all over again.

HODGKINS (louder as he tries to get Smart's attention). It sights along the wick.

SMART (to CHIEF). Maybe a lot sooner than you
think!

HODGKINS (half shouting). It fires a .22 caliber bul-
let.

SMART (half shouting back as he takes lighter). It

what?

HODGKINS (shouting). *I said it----* (SMART, pointing it L, apparently activates lighter for there is
 a bang followed by a crash of glass off L. HODG-
 KINS finishes lamely.)--fires a .22 caliber bul-
 let.

SMART (looking off L). Gee--you wouldn't think a
 .22 could do that much damage.

CHIEF (with stunned horror as he stares L). My
 aquarium! You've smashed my aquarium!

SMART. Sorry about that.

CHIEF. Don't just stand there! (Hurrying L.) My
 tropical fish!

HODGKINS (rushing off L). They're flopping on
 the floor! Water! Get water!

CHIEF (going off L). Don't step on my neon tetras!

SMART (looking after them helplessly). Gee,
 Chief----

CHIEF (shouting from off L). Max--*call for help!*

SMART (racing to desk and snatching up red telephone). Like lightning, Chief.

CHIEF (off L). Hurry!

SMART (into telephone). Emergency! Emergency!
 This is headquarters--CONTROL. We need a
 fishbowl--repeat, a fishbowl! (Listens, then:)
 Yes--you've got it. You heard right. (Puzzled.)
 Say--you sound a little like----

(CHIEF has re-entered L.)

CHIEF. *Max!*

SMART (covering telephone). Yes, Chief?

CHIEF (incredulous). You're talking into the *red*
 phone!

SMART (not registering). Yes--and it sounds like
 I'm talking to----(Suddenly realizes; gulps.)
 I'm talking to the----

CHIEF (nodding as MAX stops, hushed). The

President! (Smart's eyes widen. Then he takes a breath, clears his throat, and talks into telephone.)

SMART. Sorry--wrong number. (SMART slams down the telephone and tries to collect himself. In the distance a siren begins to sound. An alarm bell also begins ringing.)

CHIEF (seething). Not only the President--you've alerted the Pentagon--Polaris submarines-- they'll be scrambling at SAC bases all over the world.

SMART (patting the red telephone). Very efficient. Well--I better get along to the bus station.

CHIEF (containing himself). That's right, Max-- and remember the code. New York Mets win double-header.

SMART (with weak laugh). Very good, Chief. (Backing away R.) I'd like to see the day that would happen.

HODGKINS (calling from off L). Got everything but the guppies, Chief.

CHIEF (calling back L). Coming----(Forcing himself to speak calmly to SMART.) Your first stop is the bus station--and don't forget the recognition signal. (The CHIEF expels his pent up breath and hurries off L. SMART looks after him unhappily for a moment, then turns and starts off R. The light begins to dim off.)

SMART (as he goes off R, repeating to himself so he won't forget). New York Mets win double-header. (The lights have dimmed out and in the darkness the siren and bells continue for a moment and then fade out.)

(As soon as the alarms fade out, a matter-of-fact VOICE is heard announcing a bus departure. If possible the VOICE should come over a P.A., but an actor may simply call it out from backstage.)

VOICE. Bus now loading on platform seven, leav-
ing Washington, D. C. at four-fifty with stops in
Baltimore, Philadelphia, and terminating in New
York City. Bus now loading on platform seven.

(During the blackout the curtains have closed, and
the lights now come up in front of the curtains.
D R are lockers such as are used in bus termi-
nals for checking luggage. The top compartment
has a large number "13" on it. The compart-
ments below are numbered 14 and 15.)

(A MAN and a WOMAN are coming on D L. They are
dressed for travel and the MAN carries a suitcase along with a small portable radio. They are
crossing R.)

WOMAN. It's embarrassing to walk into a bus sta-
tion with someone listening to a transistor radio.
MAN. It's off. I turned it off. (Defensively.) I
couldn't believe what I was hearing, that's all.
WOMAN. You were just listening to a baseball
game.
MAN (stopping). But didn't you hear?
WOMAN. Hear what?
MAN. What happened at Shea Stadium in New York?
WOMAN (disgusted). Shea Stadium. Come on.
We'll miss our bus. (Hurries R.)
MAN (following her). Mildred--the New York Mets
just won a double-header!
WOMAN (as she exits). So?
MAN. Are you listening? The *Mets!*

(As they go off R, GARTH, a large, dangerous-look-
ing thug, comes on D L, glances about quickly,

then calls back off L.)

GARTH (hushed). Mr. Big--Mr. Big!

(A beautiful tall GIRL, whose make-up and costume
    at least suggest a Chinese origin, steps on stage
    L and faces front watchfully. Another beautiful
    tall GIRL followed by a third GIRL also come on
    L, taking up positions next to each other. They
    all have similar make-up and costumes, which
    may be as extreme as desired. Each GIRL
    stares intently in front of her, and without mov-
    ing her head--and as dead-pan as possible--each
    calls L.)

FIRST GIRL. No enemy in sight my sector. Mary
    Wong reporting.
SECOND GIRL. No CONTROL agents my sector.
    Shirley Wong reporting.
THIRD GIRL. Looks like an ordinary bus station to
    me. Betsy reporting.
GARTH (sharply). Betsy who?
THIRD GIRL (still dead-pan). Betsy *Wong* report-
    ing.
GARTH. That's better. (Calling off L again.) All
    clear, Mr. Big.

(At this MR. BIG walks on L, emerging from be-
    hind the immobile Wong girls. MR. BIG is im-
    maculately groomed, urbane, poised and charm-
    ing. He is also the smallest actor available to
    play the part.)

MR. BIG (with satisfaction). So far--perfect.
GARTH (worried). Perfect? I'm *sure* they've no-
    ticed you dropped out of sight in Hong Kong ten
    days ago.

MR. BIG. I *wanted* them to notice.

GARTH (more worried). Exposing yourself this
    way, they may even start suspecting you're
    here in Washington.

MR. BIG. I *want* them to suspect.

GARTH. But the bus station across the street
    from the Hotel Cramley!

MR. BIG (smiling). *Perfect!*

GARTH (nervously). Mr. Big, I understand there's
    something peculiar going on right now at CON-
    TROL headquarters.

MR. BIG. I wouldn't say something peculiar. I'd
    say something--fishy. (Smiles at his little joke,
    then becomes suddenly stern.) You know what
    you're to do.

GARTH (grimly). Yes, Mr. Big.

SHIRLEY WONG (dead-pan). Suspected CONTROL
    agent getting out of taxi and approaching bus
    terminal.

GARTH (with relish). Leave him to me.

MR. BIG. That's what we're doing. (To the girls.)
    All right, we activate the next Hotel Cramley
    phase of this KAOS operation--*move!* (One by
    one the girls dart off L. Then MR. BIG adjusts
    his tie and strolls off L after them. GARTH
    pulls a newspaper from inside his coat and hides
    behind it as he pretends to read.)

(Two Girls, BIG SISTER and LITTLE SISTER, are
    strolling on R, each carrying a small suitcase.)

LITTLE SISTER. I can't wait to get back to New
    York. Know what I just heard?

BIG SISTER. The smog blew away and somebody
    saw the sun. I wonder where's platform seven.

LITTLE SISTER. The Mets won a double-header.

BIG SISTER (tapping GARTH on arm). Could you

tell me where's platform seven?
GARTH (holding paper closer around his face). I
    don't know anything.
BIG SISTER (to LITTLE SISTER). Wait here while
    I ask information.
LITTLE SISTER (calling after BIG SISTER, who is
    going off L). Get a late edition, will you? Some-
    thing with a sport section?

(SMART is strolling on R, very casually, dressed
    in a business suit and a shirt with French cuffs.)

LITTLE SISTER (to GARTH). Whaddaya know, the
    Mets won a double-header! (GARTH pulls away.
    SMART stops short, registers, and then approach-
    es LITTLE SISTER cautiously.)
SMART (out of the side of his mouth). Did I hear you
    right? The Mets win double-header? (He winks.)
LITTLE SISTER (winking back). That's right.
SMART. Any new developments from KAOS?
LITTLE SISTER (baffled). The only development--
    they must've got a little hitting.
SMART (confidentially). What about the blondes?
LITTLE SISTER (indignant). If they're getting hits,
    what difference does the color of their hair make?
SMART (confused). But aren't you ninety-nine?

(BIG SISTER re-enters L, carrying a newspaper.)

LITTLE SISTER. No--I'm fourteen and a half.
BIG SISTER (calling). Platform seven is this way.
LITTLE SISTER (crossing). Anything in the paper?
BIG SISTER (as they exit L). You're right. The
    Mets took both games.

(A lovely young GIRL in a trench coat and hat comes
    on R.)

SMART (putting hand to his head as he realizes).
  They *did* win a double-header. (The girl,
  AGENT 99, has come up quietly behind SMART.
  GARTH is watching, his face not entirely con-
  cealed now by the newspaper.)

99 (softly). That's right--they won both games.

SMART (without looking, he waves her away, mut-
  tering). I know--I know. Stupid ball team--
  you can't even count on them to lose.

99. You don't understand. The score was *ninety-
  nine* to *eighty-six*.

SMART. That's ridiculous. Baseball scores are
  never--uh--oh----(Pointing to her.) 99?

99 (nodding and pointing to him). 86?

SMART (nodding). Say--you're a girl.

99 (pleased). You noticed.

SMART (appreciating her). As a matter of fact----
  (Catches himself and gets back to business.)
  Have you noticed anything suspicious, 99?

99 (bothered). So many suspicious things it's making me--well, suspicious.

SMART. Could you give that to me again, 99?

99. It's almost as though they're *wanting* us to
  suspect.

SMART. They're beginning to slip up, that's all.
  They've kidnaped too many blondes out of this
  one area.

99. That's what I mean.

SMART (still not understanding her). I better check
  in with 44 at the University, then get over to the
  Hotel Cramley before--hold it.

99 (hushed). What is it?

SMART. There's someone observing us. Take a
  look.

99. Where?

SMART. Don't turn around. Look in my mirror
  cuff links. (SMART holds up his cuff so that 99

can presumably see the reflection of GARTH, who has taken a step toward them and frozen in that position.)

99. Who is he?

SMART. Probably part of a reception committee from KAOS.

99. What are you going to do?

SMART. You divert him for just a moment. (With relish.) While I use my locker key. (99 nods, and as SMART crosses R to the locker, she crosses to GARTH.)

99. Pardon me, sir, but could you tell me where I'll find platform seven?

GARTH (pulling paper close around his face again, aggrieved). I don't know nothing about platform seven--*nothing!*

(Meanwhile SMART has come up to the locker, taken out his key, and apparently unlocked the top compartment marked 13. As the locker door is swung open, a face is seen just inside.)

SMART (out of the side of his mouth). Agent 13?

13. Yes, 86.

SMART. Man behind me. Gun under his arm. Probably KAOS agent. Put plan Y-14 into effect. 99 and I will decoy him in. All right?

13. All right. (SMART shuts locker door and crosses toward 99, who has taken several steps toward him. GARTH is peering from behind his paper again.)

SMART (in loud voice to 99). Okay, I think we better get going. There's something v-e-r-y interesting I want to show you.

99 (as SMART leads her R). This way?

SMART (as they're going). This way.

99. And you'll show me something v-e-r-y interest-

ing? (GARTH is hooked, and is following.)
SMART (as they go off R). *V-e-r-y* interesting!

(GARTH pauses right by the locker, reaching to
take out his gun. The locker door swings open,
AGENT 13 reaches out with what is apparently
a blackjack, which he brings down on Garth's
head. GARTH collapses onto the floor. SMART
steps back on R again with 99. The lights are
dimming.)

SMART (gesturing toward GARTH for 99 to see).
How about that! (Aside, to 13.) Good hunting,
13.
13 (well satisfied with himself, as he closes locker
door). Works like a charm.
SMART (to 99). The old locker trick. That's the
second time this month. Come on----

(As they go off, the lights have dimmed to black.
In the darkness a telephone starts ringing, and
it continues for a moment. The ringing stops
and light comes up in front of the curtain at L.
A large trash can has been placed on stage L,
and the four STUDENTS seen at the beginning of
the play are lined up, shamefaced, being repri-
manded by PROFESSOR ZALINKA. Each student
is holding a bit of trash.)

ZALINKA. You don't appreciate how fortunate you
are to be able to attend Professor Dante's dem-
onstrations. This messiness is inexcusable.
The lecture scheduled for this afternoon is can-
celed.
MYRA. We're sorry, Professor Zalinka.
HELEN. Look--we've gathered up all the trash.
JANE. I was about to put it in the trash can even

before you mentioned it.

ZALINKA (indignantly). Professor Dante's labora-
tory--and you're filling the ash trays to over-
flowing: empty Coke bottles, used tissues----

FRED. We *said* we're sorry.

HELEN. We've picked up everything. There's no
reason to cancel the lecture.

ZALINKA. It's canceled. Go home. Go home
right now! (With this, ZALINKA walks off L.
The students look after her for a moment and
shrug.)

MYRA. She never got mad at the mess before.

HELEN. If you ask me, she was just looking for
an excuse to tell us off.

JANE. Anyway--the lecture's canceled.

HELEN. So we'll go home. Or maybe we could
see if the Fortune Cookie Club is open this early.

MYRA. The Fortune Cookie Club is always open.
Come on--let's get rid of this trash. (As they
start out L, they drop the trash they've collect-
ed into the trash can.)

FRED. Did you hear a phone ringing a little while
ago?

JANE. Couldn't be--there's no phone in here.
(They've finished emptying their trash into the
trash can and are going off L. Light is coming
up in front of the curtain R.)

FRED (the last one to exit L). Sounded like a phone
to me.

(SMART is revealed by the light coming up R. [The
locker and Garth have gone off R during the darkness.] He is on one knee, holding his shoe-phone
to his ear. 99 is standing beside him.)

SMART (irritated). I better dial again. There's no

answer from 44. (He begins dialing, apparently some mechanism in his shoe.)

99 (worried). 44 *must* be there. He's the only one on guard now at the laboratory!

SMART (grimly). If he's allowed himself to be decoyed away from the Inthermo, I'll *break* him! (A telephone begins ringing again L.)

99. But you're in charge. He'd never move--not without direct orders from you.

SMART. Then why doesn't he answer?

(At this, a woebegone 44 rises slowly out of the trash can, with some of the litter just dumped on him probably still on his head and shoulders. He is holding a telephone to his ear, and the ringing has stopped.)

44 (emotionally) 44 here.

SMART (into telephone). About time, 44. Have you got anything?

44 (fighting to keep from crying). I've got claustrophobia.

SMART (soothing). Now, now----

44 (trying to brush off some of the trash with his free hand). You wouldn't believe the stuff that gets dumped on me!

SMART (sharply). Don't *whimper!*

44 (repressing a sob, bravely). I'm trying to get hold of myself, 86. Do *you* have anything?

SMART. About what?

44. About my relief.

SMART. The pressure's on, 44, and we're spread thin.

44. You mean----(Bites back tears.) --*no* relief?

SMART. I wish I could change places with you, but I have to guard some blonde Scandinavian princess.

99 (aside to SMART). Warn him to be careful.
I'm *sure* KAOS is planning something major.

44. Look, 86, if you'd *really* like to change places
with me----

SMART. No time, 44. I'm hanging up now and
proceeding to Hotel Cramley. Consider yourself on intermediate alert.

44 (a wail). I'm not up to an intermediate alert.
I'm not even up to----

SMART. Steady, man. I'll get back to you as soon
as I can. Meanwhile, remember--American secret agents don't whimper! (44 takes a quick
breath, but manages to control himself. With a
shrug of resignation, he sinks back down into the
trash can as the light dims out on that side of the
stage. Meanwhile, SMART is putting his shoe
back on, half leaning against 99 for support as
he does. In spite of herself, 99 is affected by
this contact with the famous Maxwell Smart.)
Excuse me.

99. *Quite* all right, 86--Mr. Smart--Max.

SMART (a gentle reprimand). We're on duty, 99.

99 (embarrassed). Yes, 86. Of course, 86. (All
business.) If you'd like to go out to the University to help 44, I'm sure I can manage with
Princess Ingrid.

SMART. The Chief figures I'm the only one who
can deal with the Princess.

99 (admiring). He must have tremendous confidence
in you.

SMART (pleased). Let's get over to the Cramley.

99 (as they start R). I've a hunch those four kidnaped blondes may still be in the vicinity.

SMART (going R). I just can't figure KAOS on this
one. (As they go off R, the curtain rises again.)

SCENE: At U R C is a suggestion of a hotel room

with several chairs and a small table on which
is a telephone. At L C is a standing screen
which may be decorated with a suggestion of
Chinese art. There are four straight-back chairs
in front of the screen and another small table on
which there is also a telephone. Actually this
screen has been placed so that it at least partial-
ly masks the CONTROL office which still stands
behind it.)

AT RISE OF CURTAIN: The emphasis of the lights
is entirely on stage R. The area at L is in semi-
darkness. A moment after the curtain goes up,
MARY WONG, followed by SHIRLEY WONG, and
then BETSY WONG all dart onto the stage from
D R, take various positions in the room U R C,
and freeze in those positions while they listen.
MARY WONG decides they can proceed.)

MARY WONG (interpreting what she's heard, in a
hushed voice to the others). She's changing her
clothes. Get busy.
SHIRLEY WONG. Everything according to plan?
BETSY WONG. Right. (Gestures to MARY.) Your
move next.
ΛARY WONG (stepping U R and calling off R).
Princess Ingrid--Princess--I'm your special
maid, assigned by the hotel. (Going off U R.)
Perhaps I can help you.

As MARY WONG goes off, the other two go into
carefully rehearsed activity. SHIRLEY WONG
unrolls a large, gaudy poster which she quickly
mounts--either with tacks or tape. One way or
another, it should be placed conspicuously and
without delay. The poster is a bright advertise-
ment for the Fortune Cookie Club. It should

suggest that this is where the action is and mention that it's located near the University. Meanwhile BETSY WONG sets a small bowl she's been
carrying on the table, also places a leaflet there,
and puts some book matches by an ash tray. As
they are finishing, and this should all be done
quickly, MARY WONG comes back on U R, calling
back off R as she comes.)

MARY WONG (calling off R). You're entirely welcome, Princess Ingrid--a pleasure to serve you.
(Glances at the others quickly to be sure they're
ready, then turns and calls R again.) One other
thing, Princess. If you can take a little time
from official business and enjoy yourself, there's
a wild crazy place out by the University. It's fab-
ulous! Just jump in a taxi and say--The Fortune
Cookie Club! (MARY WONG steps back after saying this, turns and gestures to the others. SHIR-
LEY WONG darts to D R where she freezes, and
BETSY WONG darts to the table where she picks
up the telephone. MARY WONG watches off U R
for Princess Ingrid.)
BETSY WONG (into telephone, softly). Switchboard
--I'd like to be connected with another room here
in the hotel. Would you ring suite 203, please?

(There is a ring at L. GARTH comes on quickly and
answers the telephone. He is now wearing a bandage where he was bashed.)

GARTH (into telephone). Suite 203.
BETSY WONG (continuing into telephone, softly).
Phase Three completed. Proceeding to Phase
Four. Betsy reporting.
GARTH (sharply). Betsy who?
BETSY WONG (hushed but irritated). *Wong,* idiot!

(She hangs up softly, then darts out D R. MARY
WONG darts out after her, followed by SHIRLEY
WONG. Meanwhile, GARTH has hung up, touched
his bandage and winced. He shakes his head to
clear it, and calls off L.)

GARTH. Okay, you blondes. In here and sit down.

(Four girls, ANN, JILL, MAY and LAURA, all with
light brown or blonde hair, come on L. They are
more curious than frightened.)

JILL. There has to be some rational explanation.

ANN (to GARTH). Are you finally going to explain?

MAY (also to GARTH). We're not making trouble.
We'd just like to know what's happening.

GARTH. Sit down.

LAURA. But we're going nuts--no TV, no record
player, not even a radio.

GARTH. *Sit!* (They all sit quickly at this sharp
command. The effort of giving it, however,
makes GARTH wince and touch his bandage a-
gain.)

ANN (pleasantly). Somebody give you a belt, mis-
ter?

JILL. Maybe you'd like me to run out for some
aspirin.

GARTH. Please.

MAY. What happened to the three Dragon Ladies?

GARTH. They're busy. Now listen----

LAURA. Couldn't we at least have a radio or something to pass the time? The one thing we seem
to have in common--we all like the same music.

GARTH. I know. Each one of you was observed
buying the identical record album at the music
store next to the hotel.

MAY. *Everybody* buys that singer. He's the thing
now! Terrific!

JILL. If this has something to do with our buying
    that record album, you might as well go after
    every other girl in town, too.
ANN (to the other girls). Maybe it's some kind of
    publicity stunt!
GARTH. Not a publicity stunt--but I do have a copy
    of that record--if you'd care to hear it.
LAURA. *If* we'd care to hear it!
MAY. Sure be better than staring at these walls.
GARTH. Okay, but *I* don't want to hear it. (They
    groan.) However--I have some earphones, and
    I can plug them into the turntable amplifier.
    You can hear it through the earphones.
JILL. Great.
GARTH (hesitating). You're really eager to hear
    this singer?
LAURA. Haven't we told you?
GARTH (going off L). Then just sit quietly while I
    get this rigged.
ANN (softly to the others as GARTH goes). It *is*
    some kind of publicity stunt.
MAY. If we want to get out of here soon, we better
    play along with it.
JILL. Right. We better be very appreciative.
LAURA. Nothing hard about that, is there? (The
    girls look at each other for a moment and nod.
    They're in complete agreement. Then they sit
    back, waiting for their treat.)

(There is a knock heard from off R, which is re-
    peated. Then SMART, followed by 99, comes
    on hesitantly, D R.)

SMART (calling). Hello--anyone here?
PRINCESS (calling back from off U R). Come in--
    the door's open.
SMART (to 99, disapproving). The door's open.

99. No security at all.

PRINCESS (off UR). Who is it?

SMART. Uh--an old friend.

PRINCESS (off UR). I'll be out in a moment.

99 (as they move into room). I remember the briefing now. You knew the Princess before.

SMART. We met five years ago, when she was here
with her father and I--uh----

99 (filling in as he hesitates modestly). Saved his
life.

SMART (conceding). It was one of my good days.

99. What's the Princess like?

SMART. Last time I saw her was five years ago.
She was a sweet, freckle-faced fifteen-year-old
kid.

99. She won't want to sit around. What do you plan
to do with her?

SMART. Show her the sights--places of historical
significance.

99. What if she isn't interested?

SMART. What sweet, freckle-faced kid wouldn't
want to see the sights?

(At this PRINCESS INGRID enters UR. She is tall,
blonde, Nordic, gay and vivacious.)

PRINCESS. Max! How wonderful! (She throws her
arms around him and kisses him.)

SMART. How are you, Ingrid? You haven't changed
a bit.

99 (out of the corner of her mouth to SMART, dubiously). She must have been some fifteen-year-
old.

SMART. Princess, I'd like you to meet Agent 99.
We've been assigned to escort you around Washington.

PRINCESS (hesitating). Where did you want to take

me?

SMART. We'll see all the important monuments,
    the shrines----

PRINCESS (dismayed). Monuments, shrines----

99 (aside to SMART). Careful, 86.

SMART (going right on, cheerfully). Libraries, too.

PRINCESS. No. Absolutely not.

SMART (startled). *Not?*

PRINCESS. Max, I haven't been to Washington in
    five years. I haven't been anywhere in five years.
    I'd like to enjoy myself.

SMART (baffled). Where would you like to go?

PRINCESS (trying to recall). I was told some place
    --I'd like to go to----(She sees the poster and
    points to it.) There--that's the place!

SMART (with distaste). The Fortune Cookie Club?

PRINCESS (slumping into chair). It sounds like fun.

(On the other side of the stage GARTH re-enters L,
    carrying earphones which he distributes to the
    four seated girls, who proceed with putting them
    on.)

99. I've never heard of the place.

PRINCESS. Never heard of it! (Holding up match-
    book she's taken from beside the ash tray.) Look
    at this--even the matchbook tells about it! (Pick-
    ing up leaflet.) And this leaflet--do the latest
    dances--music till dawn!

SMART. A place for college kids, Princess. (Pass-
    ing bowl from table.) Have some crackers, and
    we'll figure out an interesting itinerary.

PRINCESS (reaching into bowl absently). Who has
    more fun than college kids. (Pauses with her
    hand still in the bowl.) Max, there's something
    in this cracker.

SMART (instantly alert). *In* it?

PRINCESS (taking it from bowl). A bit of paper.

99 (puzzled). Why would there be fortune cookies here?

PRINCESS (looking at paper). Listen----(Reading.) "For the time of your life come to the----"

SMART (cutting in). Never mind. I can guess.

PRINCESS (laughing). Right. Oh, Max--this is irresistible. We *must* go!

99 (pulling SMART aside). There's something wrong, 86--or the Hotel Cramley owns a piece of the Fortune Cookie Club.

SMART. Exactly. I'll entice her into going somewhere else.

PRINCESS (calling). Max--really!

99 (concerned). She's pretty excited about----

SMART. Leave this in the capable hands of Maxwell Smart. (Turns.) Princess--The Fortune Cookie Club is out--we're going to some *real* swinging places!

PRINCESS (dubiously). Such as?

SMART. We'll start with the Washington Monument. Then the Smithsonian Institute--*wow!*

PRINCESS. I see. (Turns.) Agent 99. I'd appreciate it if you'd get my green coat. You'll find it in one of the closets.

99. Yes, of course.

(99 goes out U R. At the same time MR. BIG is coming on D L. He is holding a small metal device to one ear as he crosses to the table.)

PRINCESS. Now, Max--describe the places we'll visit. I want to visualize them.

SMART (looking off as he considers). Let me think how to begin----(In the other room JILL pulls an earphone away from her ear.)

JILL. What's happening? With these on, I can't

hear a thing.

GARTH (sharply). *Keep* them on! (Forcing a smile.)
We're about to start the record. (Meanwhile
PRINCESS INGRID, taking advantage of Smart's
back-to-her contemplation, sneaks out D R. The
moment JILL has replaced earphones, GARTH
speaks to MR. BIG.) Our bug in room 201 coming in loud and clear?

MR. BIG (nodding, indicating metal device). Everything is exactly on schedule. Better stand by the
record player. (GARTH nods and hurries off L.)

SMART. First we'll visualize that fascinating place,
the Smithsonian. Think of early airplanes, an-
tique automobiles, out-of-date typewriters,
eighteenth-century weapons----(Eagerly.) Are
you seeing it?

(99 comes back on U R.)

99 (as she enters room). Can't find any green----
(Stops as she doesn't see princess.)

SMART (turning). I tell you, Princess, just thinking about all those antiquated museum pieces,
my heart starts thumping!

99 (stunned). She's gone! 86, she's *gone!*

SMART (looking about frantically). Impossible!

99. 86--the Princess isn't here!

SMART (rushing off R). Maybe she just stepped out
in the hall.

MR. BIG (with the device at his ear, beaming).
Beautiful! Beautiful!

(SMART hurries back in R.)

SMART (stricken). She isn't there!

MR. BIG (calling L). Ready with the record player.

GARTH (from off L). Watching for your signal, Mr.

Big.

MR. BIG (picking up telephone). Switchboard, con-
nect me with room 201, please.

SMART (horrified). You don't suppose KAOS
could've----

99. She went of her own accord.

SMART. What makes you think----

99. There was no green coat. (Pointing to poster.)
She slipped out to go to the Fortune Cookie Club.
(The telephone is ringing.)

SMART. Irresponsible freckle-faced kid! (Picking
up telephone.) Now *we'll* have to slip out and go
to the----(Into telephone.) Hello.

MR. BIG. Maxwell Smart?

SMART. Speaking. (Then does "take" at this use
of his name. Cautiously.) *Who* did you want?

MR. BIG. Let's not play games, Mr. Smart. Or
would you like me to call you "86"?

SMART (covering mouthpiece, urgently to 99). It's
KAOS!

MR. BIG (sharply). Pay attention. You can talk
to 99 later.

SMART. What gives you the idea that 99----

MR. BIG. Cut the games and listen!

SMART. Sorry, friend, but I'm in a hurry. I've
no time to----

MR. BIG. You're *not* in a hurry.

SMART. I've dealt with KAOS agents before and if
you think you can----

MR. BIG. Smart--you're talking to Mr. Big!

SMART (shocked). *Mr. Big!*

99 (her lips forming the words, horrified). *Mr. Big!*

SMART (protesting into telephone). But you can't be
--Mr. Big is in Hong Kong.

MR. BIG. Ten days ago.

99 (whispering). This is bad trouble. We better
make a dash for the Fortune Cookie Club be-

fore----

SMART. Right. (Back into telephone.) Afraid I
   can't talk to you now, Big, but if you'd care to
   make an appointment----

MR. BIG (sarcastically). You're thinking of going
   out to the University--maybe stopping off at the
   Fortune Cookie Club?

SMART. As a matter of fact----

MR. BIG (emphatically). You and 99 will stay
   exactly where you are for one hour--*or else!*

SMART. Never! (Hesitating.) Or else what?

MR. BIG. We retaliate--against innocent hostages.

SMART. You wouldn't! What hostages? I don't be-
   lieve----

MR. BIG (cutting in to play an "ace"). Four--
   blonde--hostages.

SMART (covering mouthpiece, grimly). KAOS has
   the four blondes!

99 (unhappily). That's the breaks, 86. Our mission is to protect Princess Ingrid and guard the
   --you know.

SMART (back into telephone). Sorry, Big, but it
   doesn't work.

MR. BIG. Then listen while they're tortured.
   (Covers mouthpiece and calls L.) Okay, start
   the record--and I want that singer coming through
   those earphones with plenty of volume!

GARTH (from off L). The record's on, Mr. Big.

SMART (swallowing). Torture?

99 (anxiously). He wouldn't really use torture?

SMART (back into telephone). You're not scaring
   us, Big. (At this moment LAURA stands up suddenly, a look of joy on her face, clasps her hands
   with pleasure at what she is apparently hearing.
   MR. BIG is holding telephone toward them.)

LAURA (crying out happily). Ohhhhh!

SMART (misunderstanding the cry). No, no! (All

the girls have ecstatic expressions on their faces and are swaying to the music that they alone
hear. JILL comes up to her feet, too.)

JILL (apparently to some beat). Oh! Oh! Oh! Oh!

SMART (holding telephone so 99 can also hear).
You better listen, too. It's grim!

99 (hesitating). They're not really----

SMART. Yes, really----(As SMART holds telephone so 99 can also hear, the girls moan with
pleasure and MAY jumps to her feet, followed
by ANN.)

MAY (a wail of delight). He's *killing* me!

ANN (swaying, her eyes shut). I can't stand it! I
just can't stand it!

SMART (into telephone). Mr. Big--Mr. Big--no
one could be that inhuman! Not even KAOS!
(The girls wail again at what they're hearing.)
Listen to me--*stop!*

MR. BIG (also into telephone). I can make it even
worse, Smart. (MR. BIG gestures L for more
volume, which apparently comes, for the girls
let out an even louder cry of pleasure.)

SMART (deflated). Okay--we capitulate. Just stop
what you're doing to those poor girls.

MR. BIG (making a "calm down" gesture L and
turning back to telephone). Then that's it, Smart.
You and 99 stay where you are.

SMART. For one hour.

MR. BIG. And we'll release the hostages. Right?

SMART. Right. (They both hang up.)

(GARTH has come on L. The music has apparently
stopped, for the girls are calm again.)

GARTH (to MR. BIG). Did it work?

MR. BIG. Of course. Now get these girls out of
here.

GARTH (gesturing for them to move L). Come
   on----

JILL (taking off earphones). Just as I was beginning
   to enjoy myself. (Meanwhile SMART and 99 have
   been staring at each other in utter defeat.)

99 (trying to comfort SMART). There was nothing
   else you could do, 86--nothing.

SMART (unhappily). Shame on KAOS--that's like
   cheating. (The light is dimming off on area L as
   the girls, encouraged by GARTH, complete their
   exit L.)

GARTH (after them). Just sit quietly and I'll ar-
   range to let you free.

MR. BIG (to GARTH). Inform the others.

GARTH. Phase Five?

MR. BIG (nodding and starting off L). Phase Five.
   (MR. BIG exits L, followed by GARTH.)

99 (unhappily). If there was only some way we
   could protect Princess Ingrid against those fiends,
   but KAOS has thought of everything.

SMART. Not everything, 99.

99. But we don't dare move.

SMART. They may have *us* pinned down, but they
   overlooked one essential detail.

99. What detail?

SMART (reaching down to take off his shoe). Give
   me a hand, 99---- (Taking off his shoe as she
   supports him.) They've slipped up badly. (The
   lights begin to dim.)

99. How?

SMART. For one thing they made the mistake of
   challenging Maxwell Smart. And for another----
   (Turns and starts dialing his shoe-phone.) For
   another, you'll see--the last thing they expect--
   my *counter*-stroke! (The light has dimmed to
   black.)

(In the darkness the CHIEF is heard speaking, if
    possible over a public address or intercom sys-
    tem.)

CHIEF (voice only).   All departments, your atten-
    tion, please.   This is the Chief speaking from
    CONTROL headquarters.   We appear to have an
    emergency developing and all agents are request-
    ed to keep in close touch with headquarters until
    the situation is clarified.   All departments are to
    remain on stand-by alert until further notice.
    Thank you.

(The light comes up, revealing the CONTROL office
    as before--the screen, chairs, and table having
    been removed from the front of it during the black-
    out.   The CHIEF is standing behind his desk, and
    MISS FINCH is standing to the side.)

CHIEF.   With our men so overextended now, I don't
    like calling for even a standby alert, but I don't
    understand the last communication from 86, and
    there's just too much at stake.
MISS FINCH.   He's on his way in with 99 now.   (Cur-
    iously.)   Was there anything special in his last
    communication?

(SMART and 99 enter DR and begin crossing to
    DLC.)

CHIEF.   I'm sitting here bleeding for information,
    and when we finally unscramble the call from
    Smart he gives a couple of bare facts--KAOS
    has launched a major operation, they're trying
    to kidnap Princess Ingrid but don't worry, and
    ----(Picks up paper from desk and reads.)
    And quote--guess what, Chief, the Mets really

won a double-header--unquote! (SMART and 99 have turned upstage at D L C and now enter the office.)

SMART (coming in as the CHIEF concludes). How about that, Chief?

CHIEF (sharply). Smart--what happened?

SMART. The way I see it, they must've got some hitting.

CHIEF (fighting against exploding). 86--where is Princess Ingrid?

SMART. Looks to me like a KAOS trap.

CHIEF (shocked). A KAOS trap?

99. Mr. Big is directing the operation himself.

CHIEF. If it's really Mr. Big, then there's no question--KAOS is going all out.

99. They've decoyed Princess Ingrid to the Fortune Cookie Club.

CHIEF. Why didn't you go after her?

SMART. We were pinned down, but it didn't matter. Mr. Big is good, Chief, but this time he was up against old 86!

CHIEF (frantic with impatience). How were you pinned down? What did you do?

SMART (tapping his forehead). I remembered something KAOS didn't know.

CHIEF (half shouting). What?

SMART. The Fortune Cookie Club is right next to the University. KAOS sure miscalculated this time!

CHIEF (almost out of his mind). How?

SMART (the cream of the jest). They didn't realize I had another agent--*almost on the spot!*

CHIEF. What other agent? The only other agent is 44, and he's committed. He's guarding the---- (Struck by a ghastly thought.) Max--have you done something with 44? (As SMART hesitates.) Tell me! Tell me quickly, Max--*where is 44?*

SMART (has slipped off shoe and is dialing). I'm calling him right now.

CHIEF (to MISS FINCH). Stand by the emergency alert button, but don't press it till I tell you.

MISS FINCH (taking position with hand on desk mechanism). Standing by emergency alert.

99 (uneasily). 86 was under great pressure, Chief.

CHIEF (under his breath). I can feel it--I can feel what's coming!

(A sound of bright Hawaiian music is heard from off R, and the now-beaming 44, wearing several bright leis around his neck, comes on DR, holding a telephone.)

44 (turning aside, apparently so others in restaurant won't hear, half singing). This is your favorite agent, good old 44.

SMART (into shoe-phone, briskly). 86 here.

44. Good old 86.

SMART (sharply). Any sign of Princess Ingrid yet?

44. Not yet, but----

SMART (repeating to others). Not yet.

44 (continuing happily). But I'm glad to stay here just as long as you say, 86.

CHIEF (snatching shoe-phone). Give me that! (Into telephone). 44, this is the Chief.

44. Good old----(Catching himself.) I mean, yes, Chief?

CHIEF. Just tell me--*who* is on guard now at Professor Dante's laboratory?

44 (obviously). I assume 86 sent my relief. Naturally there's *someone* on guard.

CHIEF. I'm investigating, 44. Stand by for instructions.

44 (subdued, going off DR). Yes, Chief. (The music fades off as the CHIEF hands shoe back to

SMART.)
SMART (anxiously). I had to save Princess Ingrid!
   If you'd heard the cries of those tortured girls!

(HODGKINS is coming in L.)

CHIEF. What tortured girls?
99. The four kidnaped blondes
SMART. I couldn't risk Princess Ingrid being tor-
   tured, too!
HODGKINS. A report just in. The four blondes
   were released--unhurt.
SMART (bewildered). But I *heard* them!
CHIEF. They fooled you.
SMART. What possible reason----
CHIEF. Maybe they wanted you to pull 44 away
   from his post.
99 (clutching his arm). Oh, 86!
CHIEF (a furious demand). Tell me, and tell me
   fast--who is guarding the Inthermo?
SMART (miserably). You see, these girls were
   giving such terrible cries, and----
CHIEF (shouting). *Who is guarding the Inthermo?*
   (A loud voice, if possible coming over a loud-
   speaker, is heard in reply.)
VOICE. *We* are guarding the Inthermo. (Every-
   one reacts with extreme surprise, looking about
   for the source of this sound.)
HODGKINS. What was that?
99. Who spoke?
CHIEF. Where did it come from?
VOICE. KAOS. This is KAOS speaking.
CHIEF (shocked). They've planted a two-way bug!
VOICE. That's right.
CHIEF (calling up). What about the Inthermo?
VOICE. We have it, thank you. We also have
   Princess Ingrid. She took the wrong cab when

she left the hotel. Most ungallant of Mr. Smart
to let her leave unescorted. And imagine our
surprise--finding a perfect scale model of the
most powerful weapon in the world completely
unguarded!

CHIEF (calling). What do you want? What are
your terms?

VOICE. You'll hear our terms later. Meanwhile,
our thanks to Maxwell Smart. (They all turn
and look at SMART, who backs away, a look of
utter despair on his face. Suddenly SMART
starts looking through his pockets.)

CHIEF (bitterly). What are you looking for--the
fountain pen with the suicide pellet?

SMART (miserably). As a matter of fact--yes.

CHIEF (folding his arms). Go right ahead.

SMART (helpless). I can't. (The curtain is falling.)

CHIEF. Why not? Lost your nerve?

SMART (the final unhappiness). No--I've lost the
fountain pen.

CURTAIN

ACT TWO

THE HOUSELIGHTS DIM off and in the darkness a
VOICE is heard, if possible over a loudspeaker
system.)

VOICE (official-sounding, low key). CONTROL
headquarters to all personnel. CONTROL headquarters to all personnel. Full emergency alert
was declared at sixteen hundred hours. All pro-
cedures and regulations in accordance with con-
dition flash red now operational. Maximum
security precautions mandatory. Oh, and any
member of CONTROL encountering agent 86--
that's 86--tell him to call headquarters. Over
and out.

(The light is coming up in front of the curtain reveal·
ing the large trash can just onstage D L. On the
other side of the stage PROFESSOR ZALINKA is
entering D R followed by AGENTS 13 and 44.)

ZALINKA (as she strides on R). Stupid! Outra-
geous!
13. Sorry, Miss Zalinka.
ZALINKA. *Professor* Zalinka.
13 (refusing to be put down). *Associate* professor--
I just thought there might be some clue you've
overlooked.
ZALINKA. Professor Dante and I have been over
this with the FBI, the CIA, Military Intelligence,
and the Police. I'm not clear where you fit in.

44 (dropping his voice). We're *much* more secret.

ZALINKA. Obviously. Why don't you run along and let us get on with our work?

44 (hurt). What made you say--"obviously"?

ZALINKA (impatiently). I have to assist Professor Dante.

(The STUDENTS are coming on R, carrying notebooks as well as some trash.)

44. Assist him?

ZALINKA. Putting equipment away so we can go to dinner. (To STUDENTS.) I see you're finally getting the idea.

HELEN. The seminar room is cleaner than we found it. You could perform an appendectomy.

MYRA. We're getting a lot of mess from classes before us. (Quickly.) Not that I mind!

ZALINKA (pleasantly). So little trash getting in the trash cans, we almost lost our scavenger service.

JANE (giving humorous salute to 13 and 44 as she passes). You secret agents come up with anything?

13 (bristling). Who said we're secret agents?

JANE. Oh, come on.

FRED. You're like--obvious.

ZALINKA (going off L, dropping trash in can as she passes, highly amused). *He* said it.

MYRA. So much coming and going since yesterday --what's up?

44 (big gesture of innocence). What would we know?

JANE (dropping her trash in can as she goes off L). Even the secret agents don't know what's happening!

HELEN (also dropping her trash as she exits L). Frightening!

MYRA (pausing and turning back to 13). There was
    another man hanging around--but he disappeared.
13 (urgently). What other man?
MYRA. I think his name was Smart. (Dropping
    trash in can.) That's it--Max Smart.
13 (disappointed). Him. (MYRA exits L.)
FRED (volunteering). An over-age student. You
    know, one of those guys that never seems to
    graduate.
13. I'm curious. You think we're--(Laughs at
    absurdity of it.) --secret agents, but not this--
    this Smart. Why's that?
FRED (pausing at L to dump in his trash, too).
    When I asked Smart what's his line, he shot back
    --"I'm a spy"! (It's so ridiculous.) What *real*
    secret agent would say a thing like that? (FRED
    goes off L, as AGENTS 13 and 44 turn and look
    at each other, dumfounded.)
13 (a revelation). *That's* how Smart does it--he's
    so obvious, he's oblique!
44. Wait till the Chief gets his hands on him again!
    (As he goes off L.) I can't imagine where 86 is
    hiding out.
13 (following 44 off L). My hunch--Brazil.

(As they complete their exit, a telephone starts ring-
    ing L. 99 steps onstage R, anxiously clutching a
    telephone.)

99 (pleading with telephone). Come in, Max--hear
    my call--oh, please, it's important--come in,
    come in, wherever you are----

(Suddenly there is a loud disturbance from inside the
    trash can L. Then slowly, from out of the can,
    emerges the littered head and shoulders of Secret
    Agent MAXWELL SMART. Apparently his left

hand is stuck and he's struggling frantically to
free it.   Finally it comes unstuck and emerges
with his shoe-phone, which he puts to his ear.)

SMART (imitating voice of female telephone opera-
    tor).   What number are you calling, please?
99 (urgently).   The number I'm calling?   I'm try-
    ing to reach--well--86.
SMART (continuing imitation).   That number has
    been temporarily----(Hesitates as voice regis-
    ters but still suspicious.) Who's trying to reach
    86?
99.   This is 99.
SMART (his own voice).   This is 86.
99.   Max! (Faintly indignant as she collects her-
    self.) What took you so long to answer?
SMART.   Did you ever try taking off a shoe inside
    a trash can?
99.   Trash can?   You think you have to hide from
    the Chief in a trash can?
SMART.   Who's hiding?   I'm still on the job.
99.   But a trash can----(Shrugs. Who knows?)
    Have you come up with anything, 86?
SMART (nodding).   Most college students are going
    to die of lung cancer.   There's at least four inch-
    es of cigarette butts on the bottom of this----
99 (impatiently).   Anything else?   Something I could
    mention to the Chief?   I'll be seeing him in a few
    minutes.
SMART.   I'll be seeing him pretty quick myself.
99 (delighted).   You *have* come up with something!
SMART (bringing out his right hand holding some-
    thing).   Actually--the only other thing is a for-
    tune cookie.
99 (decidedly let down, but making the best of it).
    Well, see what it says--maybe it's good luck.
SMART (apparently breaking cookie, and looking at

slip, shrugging).   Some Chinese place putting out recipes.

99 (back to business). Listen, 86. I'm doing something a little crazy, and you've got to know. What it is--I want to show the Chief--I mean, *prove* that --that *anyone* can make a mistake.

(ZALINKA is coming back on L during the above speech, pauses, and regards SMART with casual curiosity.)

SMART (noticing ZALINKA but continuing casually into shoe-phone). You can tell me about it later.

99. I better tell you right now----

SMART. Right now I have company.

99. In the trash can? (Takes a breath, uneasy at situation.) Then I have to go ahead without telling you. Good luck, 86. (She goes back off R.)

SMART. Be seeing you.

ZALINKA (as SMART takes shoe from ear). Well, well--the third man. (Nods L.) Your two friends went that way. (Indicating shoe.) Or maybe you were just talking to them with your size eleven and a half telephone.

SMART. Where are you having dinner tonight?

ZALINKA. None of your----

SMART. Professor Dante *is* my business.

ZALINKA. I'm not accountable to some trash can eavesdropper!

SMART (indignantly). I was looking for----(Stops himself and finishes lamely.) I was looking.

ZALINKA (challenging contemptuously). And what have you found?

SMART. I've found----(Looks at the contents of his right hand. As he considers it an idea begins to stir. To himself:) The Fortune Cookie Club----

ZALINKA (uninterested). What?

SMART. Nothing--I found a fortune cookie, that's all.

ZALINKA (holding out her hand for it). What does it say?

SMART (still regarding broken cookie). Some kind of Chinese----(Looking more closely. To himself:) That's no recipe.

ZALINKA (pleasantly). Let me see.

SMART (closing both the subject and his right hand). Nothing to it. Don't be late for dinner. (SMART starts sinking down into trash can again.)

ZALINKA (considers further comment, but decides against it). I see. Of course.

SMART (disappearing down into trash can). Excuse me, please. (A disturbance starts from inside the trash can again. The lights begin to dim.)

ZALINKA (calling down into trash can). What are you trying to do?

SMART (from inside trash can, exasperated). I'm trying to put on my shoe! (ZALINKA shakes her head, turns and hurries off L as the disturbance caused by Smart's frantic effort continues until the light dims to black.)

(There is a brief moment of silence, and then a radio newscast is heard, during which the curtain begins to rise.)

RADIO VOICE. We conclude this network newscast with the final question put to the President at his press conference today. When asked for his reaction to the unexpected postponement of the NATO conference by the host country, Scandinavia, the President replied that he expects the technical difficulties to be cleared up--*momentarily*.

SCENE: The curtain has risen, revealing CON-
TROL headquarters occupying area at stage L
as before.)

AT RISE OF CURTAIN: The CHIEF is standing
tensely behind his desk across which he faces
99.)

CHIEF. The President put it stronger to me----
(Picking up red telephone.)--over *this!*

99. He expects us to recover Princess Ingrid--
momentarily.

CHIEF. Or the Scandinavians blow the lid off!
Meanwhile KAOS could be getting ready to *use*
the Inthermo!

99. 86 will stop them.

CHIEF. I haven't seen or talked to that idiot since
he ran out of here yesterday.

99. Running out to *do* something.

CHIEF. Until you said that, I didn't think things
could possibly get worse.

99. Chief, he has a magnificent record. You told
me yourself.

CHIEF. He had a lot of fool luck going for him,
that's all. Imagine a trained agent who can't
tell the difference between some girls who
are----(The CHIEF is interrupted by voices
coming from off L.)

VOICE (off L, a cry). Ohhhhh!

CHIEF (hesitating). Girls who are----

VOICE (off L, louder). *Ohhhhh!*

CHIEF (startled). What's that?

99. Listen--carefully.

VOICE (off L). Oh! Oh! Oh! Oh!

CHIEF. But it *sounds* like----

VOICE (off L, loud). I can't stand it! I just can't
stand it!

CHIEF (increasingly disturbed). Can't stand it?

99. What do you think, Chief?

VOICE (off L, a wail). Oh--he's *killing* me!

CHIEF. Killing! (Starting off L.) I better find out----

99 (sharply). Chief--wait!

CHIEF (hesitating). There's something terrible----

99 (darting around to the Chief's side of the desk). You're leaving your desk unguarded.

CHIEF. What are you talking about? (Another loud wail startles him into starting L again.) I've got to find out----

99 (snatching folder from desk and holding it aloft). While you find out, I get your top secret folder --for your eyes only. Suppose I was from KAOS?

CHIEF (furious, demanding). Have you lost your mind? What's happening?

99 (flipping switch on desk intercom). Hodgkins-- switch the sound from the earphones to the speaker. (There's a sudden blare from off L of the worst possible example of the latest "bad" hit music.)

CHIEF (has come up to desk and calls into inter- com). Hodgkins--cut that noise, and get in here! (The music is cut.)

99 (leaning over toward intercom). And bring the blondes.

CHIEF (beginning to understand). The blondes---- (Into intercom.) Yes--bring the blondes. (Turns and takes folder back from 99.) Now you're go- ing to explain, and I mean *right now!*

99 (retreating around desk). We had the four kid- naped girls here to tape descriptions of the KAOS personnel.

CHIEF (impatiently). Routine. What I want to know----

99 (gulping quickly). What I thought--as long as
   they were here, why not re-create the conditions of the KAOS trap--so we'll have a better
   understanding of the----
CHIEF (sharply). What you thought--you'd prove
   I could be just as big an idiot as Smart!

(HODGKINS is coming on L, shepherding the four
   blondes.)

99 (conciliatory). All I meant, Chief--*any* humane
   man----
CHIEF. This is a crisis, 99!
99 (uncowed). That's why you should keep our best
   agent on the case. (Before the CHIEF can reply.)
   Maybe he'll get lucky again.
JILL. *Every* time I start enjoying myself someone
   pulls a switch!
ANN. The way this record keeps coming up, it *has*
   to be publicity.
HODGKINS. Don't be silly. (To CHIEF.) When we
   used the earphone, they gave the predicted reaction.
CHIEF (briefly). I heard.
LAURA (to CHIEF). I'm getting so confused--are
   you one of the good guys or one of the bad guys?
CHIEF (snapping). What do you think?
99 (as LAURA flinches). He's one of the good guys,
   but right now he's in a bad temper.
MAY (indignant). We walked into a record store,
   and all of a sudden it's a federal case.
HODGKINS (wryly). With a little more luck like
   we've had, it'll reach the United Nations.
CHIEF (shortly). Hodgkins, see that the young
   ladies are suitably thanked, and have a staff car
   take them home.
JILL. What do you mean, *"suitably"*?

CHIEF (badgered). I don't know--buy them copies
　　of that terrible record.

ANN. You mean it?

JILL. I'm getting switched on again.

HODGKINS (urging them L). This way--ladies.

LAURA (as she goes). I guess you're a good guy
　　after all.

HODGKINS. Please.

MAY (calling back). That music absolutely *kills*
　　me!

CHIEF (nodding). I heard.

(As they complete exit L, MISS FINCH hurries on
　　D L, crosses to D L C, and turns to enter office.)

99 (apologetic). I'm sorry if this experiment
　　wasted even a few minutes, Chief, but I think
　　it demonstrates how KAOS----

CHIEF. Cut the nonsense, 99. We've been over
　　what it demonstrates, and if you ever pull a
　　trick like that again----(Stopping himself as
　　he sees MISS FINCH waiting.) What is it?

MISS FINCH. Sir--86 is on his way in.

CHIEF. 86! (Half to himself.) My hunch was he'd
　　gone to Brazil.

(SMART strides in D L, crosses to D L C, and turns
　　to enter office.)

99. Never!

CHIEF (conceding). I don't know. A few more
　　things go wrong, *I'll* go to Brazil.

SMART (coming up to desk). Before you say a word,
　　Chief, I want you to know that I agree! An agent
　　who can't tell the difference between torture and
　　music appreciation has to be an absolute *idiot!*

CHIEF. Never mind, 86. Let's get on to----

SMART. But I *want* to say it--only a fool--an utter fool----

CHIEF (cutting in to close subject). Anyone can make a mistake, Max. Now let's proceed to----

SMART. But such an incredibly stupid----

CHIEF (emphatically). I said *anyone,* and the subject is dropped.

SMART (peering at him more closely, all sympathy). You've been having a tough time today, Chief--having to face all those terrible decisions with no help or advice from me.

CHIEF. And *loving* it!

SMART (ignoring Chief's comment). No need to panic! I'm back, and everything's going to be fine.

CHIEF. What've you been doing?

SMART (boyishly frank). Probably *you'd* call it hard work and shrewd deduction, but I'd just call it luck.

99 (delighted). I knew it!

CHIEF (eager in spite of himself). A stroke of luck?

SMART. I think I'm on to something.

MISS FINCH. I'm dying to hear.

SMART. So is KAOS. Chief, have you eliminated the bug they planted here?

CHIEF. A whole crew of technicians was up all night going over this office inch by inch. Wherever the bug was, it's gone. Now tell me----

SMART. For the next step I'll need 99 as part of my cover. (Stopping, uneasily.) I don't like your not finding *any* bug.

CHIEF. Neither do I, but those technicians know their business and I'm absolutely assured--there's *no* bug here. (Turns to MISS FINCH.) Check the message center, and see if anything's come in.

MISS FINCH. Right away. (SMART is taking a
    small object from his pocket.)
CHIEF (to MISS FINCH). If 13 and 44 haven't re-
    ported, put out a call. (Turning to SMART, who
    is holding up his small object.) 86----(Hesi-
    tates as he notices.) What are you doing?
SMART (indicating object--which may be any sort
    of small flashlight with a red lens; it is already
    lighted). My portable bug detector. It's sup-
    posed to show red if we're bugged.
CHIEF. It's showing red.
SMART. Then we're bugged.
MISS FINCH (as she exits D L C). Excuse me.
CHIEF (taking gadget from SMART). Let me see it.
    (MISS FINCH goes off D L.)
99 (to SMART). What sort of cover am I supposed
    to----(She stops as she sees SMART shaking his
    head with his finger to his lips.)
SMART (whispering). Didn't you hear? We're
    bugged!
CHIEF. Don't be silly.
SMART. My portable bug detector proves----
CHIEF (showing gadget which is now unlighted).
    First it was on. Now it's off. (Putting gadget
    on desk.) Can't be right both ways.
SMART (perplexed). That's really peculiar.
CHIEF. This office has been checked out with the
    most sophisticated electronic detection devices
    known. Let's get to business.

(MISS FINCH is coming back on D L, crosses to
    D L C, turns and comes into office.)

SMART. Right. Come on, 99.
CHIEF. But you haven't told me your plan?
SMART. Trust me, Chief.
CHIEF. I trusted you yesterday.

SMART. I had an off day yesterday.

CHIEF (exploding). *Off day!*

99 (diverting CHIEF to MISS FINCH). Chief, Miss Finch may have news.

CHIEF (to MISS FINCH). Anything?

MISS FINCH (nodding). A report from 13. He says all quiet.

CHIEF. Good. And 44?

MISS FINCH. He reports all quiet, too.

SMART. I don't like it.

CHIEF (irritated). Why not?

SMART. It's *too* quiet!

CHIEF. We're fighting KAOS; not the Apaches! (Bitterly sarcastic.) So unless your sixth sense is giving off sparks, I'd like a briefing on what you and 99 plan to----

SMART (cutting in). My sixth sense is giving off sparks, Chief. (Picking up gadget from desk, which, as he shows it, is seen to be lighted again.) And so is my bug detector!

CHIEF (exasperated). On--off--on! Max, it's *got* to be out of whack!

SMART (calling up into air). CONTROL calling KAOS--do you read me--over.

CHIEF (dealing with insanity). Max, listen to me. Sit down for a minute. Relax. Rest a little!

SMART (ignoring CHIEF). CONTROL calling KAOS--do you read me--over. CONTROL calling KAOS----

CHIEF (half to himself). He's cracking under the strain. He needs sedation--a psychiatrist!

SMART. CONTROL calling KAOS--do you read me? CONTROL calling KAOS----

(An ominous VOICE speaking over a loudspeaker cuts in.)

VOICE (loud and emphatic).　KAOS answering
　　CONTROL.　KAOS answering CONTROL.　We
　　read you loud and clear.　We read you loud and
　　clear.

99 (stunned).　KAOS!

CHIEF (utterly incredulous).　I don't believe it!

SMART (more nervous than proud).　Talk about a
　　sixth sense!

VOICE.　Nice of you to call us, CONTROL.　We
　　were about to call you.

CHIEF (insisting).　But they can't!　We checked
　　everything!　There's no possible way!

SMART (holding up lighted gadget, insisting). Chief,
　　we are bugged.

VOICE.　Don't worry about technicalities.　All you
　　have to do is get the message.

SMART (calling up).　Or what?

VOICE.　Or else!

SMART (regretfully).　I was afraid you'd say that.

VOICE (tough).　Now hear this.　As soon as you
　　pay the ransom we will return the Inthermo.

CHIEF.　And Princess Ingrid?

VOICE.　We hold her hostage.　If the ransom is
　　delivered as specified she'll be released, too.

CHIEF.　How much do you want?

VOICE.　One hundred million dollars.

CHIEF (staggered).　*One hundred million!*

VOICE.　*Dollars.*　And in small bills, please.
　　Fives, tens, twenties--and we'll want a few
　　singles.

CHIEF.　I could never get such a sum.　It would
　　take an act of Congress.

VOICE.　KAOS appreciates your difficulty and we
　　plan to help.　We plan a practical demonstra-
　　tion of the Inthermo's enormous power, and how
　　effectively we can use it!　Within a matter of
　　hours, we'll destroy one of your most cherished

national treasures. How's that for cooperation?

CHIEF. One of our national treasures--you wouldn't dare!

VOICE. Within a matter of hours. And if you have difficulty raising the ransom, we'll build a full-scale Inthermo and start on your state capitals.

CHIEF (taking heart). Not so fast. I've been advised you could not possibly build a full-scale Inthermo without help from Professor Dante.

VOICE. You're entirely right.

CHIEF. Then don't make empty----

VOICE (interrupting). But you see, we now *have* Professor Dante.

CHIEF (shocked). You what?

VOICE. *We* have Dante. Confirmation should be along any minute from 13. Perhaps even 44.

CHIEF (defeated). If they've got Dante, too----

SMART. Don't worry Chief. (Gestures for 99 to follow him D L C, which she does. He calls back as though to advertise his continued presence.) Remember--we've got *lots* of state capitals. (The light is beginning to dim as SMART and 99 turn and hurry off D R.)

VOICE. Only *one* thing to worry about--raising the hundred million. (The light is dimming fast.) That's in small bills, please--fives, tens, twenties--and some singles. (In the darkness, the sound of street traffic is heard briefly and then fades away to be replaced with the sound of Hawaiian music as heard earlier in connection with The Fortune Cookie Club.)

(The light comes up onstage R, revealing two or three small restaurant tables with chairs, and a suggestion of Chinese decorations. Two girls, BIG SISTER and LITTLE SISTER, are sitting at one of the tables, looking up at a large WAITER who is facing them, with his back to the audience.)

BIG SISTER. What happened to our order?

LITTLE SISTER. You're not our waiter.

WAITER. Your waiter went home. We're closing early.

BIG SISTER. Then you better hurry our order.

WAITER. We're closing.

LITTLE SISTER (reasonably). We eat at The Fortune Cookie Club every time we get back to Washington. We ordered Won Ton soup, chicken sub gum----

WAITER. The cook went home.

BIG SISTER. We've been waiting forty minutes.

LITTLE SISTER (repeating carefully). Won Ton soup, chicken sub gum, sweet and sour----

WAITER. You might as well go home, too.

BIG SISTER. After waiting forty----

WAITER (shrugging). You want to wait some more? (The two sisters start getting up.)

BIG SISTER. Wait some more!

LITTLE SISTER. Why didn't the other waiter tell us?

WAITER. He was a little confused.

LITTLE SISTER (starting off DR). He seemed fine to me.

WAITER (after them). I straightened him out.

BIG SISTER (as they go off DR). Ridiculous time to be closing!

LITTLE SISTER. Never come here again! (The WAITER turns front as they exit DR, pleased at his little joke. We see now that the WAITER is GARTH.)

GARTH (repeating to himself, highly amused). I straightened him out.

(GARTH glances after departing girls again, then
   crosses to small gong which is a part of the decorations, and strikes it. From UR the THREE
   WONG GIRLS dart in one at a time.)

MARY WONG (darting to DR). Last customers going off down street. Mary Wong reporting.
SHIRLEY WONG (darting to one of tables). Ready
   at table according to plan. Shirley Wong.
BETSY WONG (darting to position DR C). In position this side. Betsy Wong.

(Something is missing, and GARTH strikes the
   gong again. At this, PRINCESS INGRID, dressed
   like the Wong girls, and carrying a small container, darts on UR.)

PRINCESS (placing container on back table). Weap-
   on carrier in position. Ingrid reporting.
BETSY WONG (demanding). Ingrid who?
PRINCESS. Ingrid *Wong*.
GARTH. Very good.
MARY WONG (looking R). CONTROL agents 86
   and 99 approaching.
GARTH. As expected! Phase Fourteen now opera-
   tional. (GARTH goes off UR.)

(MARY WONG steps back to make way and bows as
   SMART and 99 enter cautiously DR.)

MARY WONG. Welcome to The Fortune Cookie
   Club.
SHIRLEY WONG (pulling back chairs). Won't you
   sit here, please.
99 (nervously). Quite nice, really.
SMART. I'm crazy about Chinese food.
99 (as she sits, apprehensively). There don't seem

to be any other customers.

SHIRLEY WONG. We start filling up soon. Meanwhile we can give you special service.

BETSY WONG (bringing them). Your menus.

99. Thank you.

SMART (suggesting they move back). Please--when
we need help, we'll ask.

BETSY WONG. As you wish. (The WONGS draw
back and SMART leans across table to talk to
99, who is leaning toward him.)

SMART (an urgent whisper). Notice the fortune
cookies? Exactly like the one I found in the
trash can.

99 (hushed). It had some kind of recipe.

SMART (hushed). But it *wasn't* a recipe. It was
a *formula.*

99. And that's how they transmit----(Catching
herself and pointing at menu.) Paradise Chick-
en with pineapple looks good.

SMART. I was thinking of shrimps in black bean
sauce----(Softly again.) You're right. That's
how they transmit. Who checks on the international flow of fortune cookies? (Looking about
cautiously.) I'm sure this is a KAOS front.

99. Notice anything special?

SMART (with a cautious nod). Something a little
peculiar about the fourth Chinese waitress.

99 (without turning). What did you notice that's
peculiar?

SMART. I noticed that the fourth Chinese waitress
is a blue-eyed blonde.

99 (concerned). When this is over, you should take
a real vacation, Max. (Glances casually at
INGRID, then back to SMART.) We'll both need
a vacation.

SMART (motioning her closer). Let's recapitulate
the basic plan. (As 99 leans very clo, e, MARY

WONG signals to the others and they dart over
to where PRINCESS INGRID stands near the
weapons container, out of which they arm them-
selves.)

99. Synchronize timers?

SMART (nods, and they both press buttons on their
watches). At oh-two minutes, you get up to telephone, but actually you head for the kitchen. At
oh-three minutes, I try to look into the basement
while you create a diversion complaining about
sanitary conditions. At oh-four minutes I come
back from the basement, and at oh-five min-
utes----(SMART stops himself as he becomes
aware of the three Wong girls and PRINCESS
INGRID, who have come up in a semi-circle behind them, armed with all the weapons they can
carry. He looks from the battle-ready WONGS
back to 99. Casually.) This may put us a *little*
behind schedule.

MARY WONG (quietly but with deadly firmness).
You will slowly place your hands together in back
of your chairs.

SMART (as he complies). The old Chinese waitress
trick. That's the third time this year.

MARY WONG (gesturing to others). Tie their hands.
Make them as uncomfortable as possible. (SHIR-
LEY and BETSY WONG dart forward and start
securing SMART and 99 to their chairs.)

99 (during this, regretfully). I was beginning to
want some of that Paradise Chicken.

SMART. Not me--shrimps.

99. What I love are those undercooked pea pods,
bamboo shoots, water chestnuts----

SHIRLEY WONG (interrupting as she ties 99, apolo-
getically). The kitchen is closed.

99. I'm so sorry.

SHIRLEY WONG. Would you mind holding a finger

over the knot?

99 (apparently doing so). Glad to----

SHIRLEY WONG (finishing). Thank you.

BETSY WONG (pulling hard, apparently to tighten knot tying Smart's hands). Is that quite painful?

SMART (calmly). Excruciating.

BETSY WONG. If the rope was a little thinner, I could make it agonizing.

SMART. Maybe next time.

MARY WONG. Proceed to Phase Fifteen. (Points to PRINCESS.) You guard the prisoners. (PRINCESS steps backward to a high stool U R C, where she sits watchfully, gun in hand.) I inform Mr. Big. (To others.) You start preparing speedboat. (SHIRLEY and BETSY WONG dart out U R, followed by MARY WONG. PRINCESS raises whatever weapon she holds, guarding SMART and 99 who are faced away from her.)

99 (softly). Did you hear, 86--*Mr. Big!*

SMART (conceding in whisper). We hit the jackpot!

99. For the first time, I think I'm afraid.

SMART. The first time *ever*, or the first time *today?*

99. The first time since I started working with you.

SMART. Listen, 99. A coward is a frightened man who's scared to be brave. A brave man is only a coward who isn't scared of being frightened.

99 (uncertainly). Thank you, Max. I'll remember that.

(MR. BIG has come on U R, crossing to where he faces his captives.)

MR. BIG. So--we meet at last. What an unexpected and delightful pleasure to have the illustrious Maxwell Smart as my guest----(Looking toward 99.) I see that what your organization lacks in strategy it more than makes up for in loveliness.

SMART (accepting compliment with slight bow).
Thank you.

99. May we ask the name of our--well, host?

MR. BIG. But of course. I'm Mr. Big.

99 (unprepared for his small size). *You* are----

SMART (as MR. BIG nods). It's all in his dossier.

99 (impelled by curiosity). If you don't mind one
more question, who gave you the name--Big?

MR. BIG. My psychiatrist. (Rubbing hands together with pleasure.) We've planned an amus-
ing little divertissement that will shock and hor-
rify you as it will every American. In a matter
of hours we will prove that your government is
defenseless against the power of KAOS.

99. What are you going to do?

MR. BIG. Destroy the Statue of Liberty.

SMART. Maybe you should try a different psychiatrist.

MR. BIG. We'll come up on the statue in a way
no one expects--then activate the Inthermo!

SMART. We know all about your plan.

MR. BIG (a smiling challenge). Can you mention
even one detail?

SMART. Certainly. You plan to come up on the
statue in a *speedboat*--a way everyone expects.

MR. BIG (stepping back, startled). What?

SMART (pushing his apparent advantage). Listen,
my charming little friend, at this very moment
there are seven Coast Guard cutters getting ready
to converge on your speedboat. Would you believe it? Seven!

MR. BIG (as he considers, frankly). I find that
pretty hard to believe.

SMART (after brief pause, trying to be reasonable).
Would you believe six?

MR. BIG (sure of himself again). You're bluffing,

Mr. Smart, but I'm not-.---(Grimly.) As your
    country is about to discover!
SMART (warning). If KAOS takes this step, we re-
    taliate!
MR. BIG. How? We've got the Inthermo, and
    we've got Professor Dante.
SMART. Suppose we get help from Dante's assist-
    ant? Then we build an Inthermo, too!
MR. BIG (calling UR). Dear--would you come in,
    please.
SMART. Listen to me, Big!
MR. BIG. You were saying?

(ZALINKA, wearing a sophisticated outfit, is com-
    ing on UR.)

SMART (continuing passionately). Why go on with
    this senseless escalation? All we'll achieve is
    a balance of terror! You with your Inthermo!
    We with our----(Stops as she registers.)
    Zalinka!
ZALINKA. That's right.
SMART (nodding toward MR. BIG). You're with----
ZALINKA (cheerfully nodding). Right again.
SMART (drained, looking toward MR. BIG again).
    How was it you said you wanted the hundred mil-
    lion?
MR. BIG. I'll communicate details right after our
    little demonstration--not that they'll matter to
    you. (To ZALINKA.) Professor Dante is to
    see the prisoners.
ZALINKA. He's being brought up now.
99 (aside to SMART). No wonder it was easy for
    them to kidnap the Professor.
SMART. And the trap they set for us here--she
    saw me with the fortune cookie. (To ZALINKA.)
    I'll be frank. I'm disappointed in you.

(PROFESSOR DANTE comes on U R with GARTH,
    who has hold of his arm.)

DANTE (pushing Garth's hand away). You're hurt-
    ing me.
MR. BIG (to GARTH). Professor Dante is our
    guest. He's going to build us a full-scale In-
    thermo. (Unctuously.) And we're going to give
    him anything he wants.
DANTE. All I want is some Paradise Chicken, and
    to go home.
MR. BIG. I'm afraid you can't go home.
DANTE. The government will be sending someone
    to look for me.
MR. BIG. They already sent someone to look for
    you. (Indicating SMART and 99.) And here they
    are. They are our guests, too.
SMART. Hello, Professor. The service here is
    terrible.
DANTE (to SMART and 99). You're captives?
99. Thanks to your ex-assistant.
GARTH (to MR. BIG). Time's getting short.
MR. BIG (to DANTE). You see--no one is coming
    to the rescue. So be realistic. Cooperate.
DANTE (to himself). I should've gone to an Italian
    restaurant.
MR. BIG (to GARTH). Escort him to his room,
    then move at once to Phase Sixteen.
ZALINKA (starting U R). I better make sure the
    Inthermo is ready to move.
MR. BIG. We push off in six minutes. (ZALINKA
    goes off U R.)
GARTH (urging DANTE U R). This way--we're in
    a hurry.
99 (calling to DANTE). Professor--they're using
    your Inthermo to blow up the Statue of Liberty!
DANTE (stopping short). The *Statue of Liberty!*

GARTH. Come on! I have to see you to your room!

DANTE. But my great-grandparents! Their first sight of America!

MR. BIG (sharply). Five minutes and forty seconds!

DANTE (as he is half-dragged off UR bv GARTH). It says--"Give me your tired, your poor, your huddled masses yearning to breathe free"--and you want to blow it up with *my* Inthermo!

MR. BIG (calling after him). Exactly!

SMART (to MR. BIG). What about us? You're just going to leave us here?

MR. BIG. Under a very special guard. (Delighted.) Actually this is one of my favorite parts of the whole operation. (Turns to PRINCESS INGRID, who has remained on her high stool UR C.) Come meet your prisoners. (Back to SMART and 99.) You're going to love this, too.

SMART (as PRINCESS comes into his field ot vision). The blue-eyed blonde Chinese.

MR. BIG (a whispered aside to them). Recently from Scandinavia.

99 (realizing). Princess Ingrid.

MR. BIG (to PRINCESS). What's your name?

PRINCESS (shrugging at the foolish question). Ingrid Wong.

99. Wong?

SMART (sharply). Your name isn't Wong!

PRINCESS (pointing gun at SMART). Don't try to move.

99. Where are you from? Where was your home?

PRINCESS (to MR. BIG). Should I answer?

MR. BIG. Go ahead.

PRINCESS. Hong Kong.

SMART (furious). What've you done to her?

MR. BIG. Part brainwashing. Part hypnotism. It's a new technique I developed--so good I'm leaving *her* to guard you! (As he is going off UR.) Isn't

that delicious? (The moment MR. BIG is off,
SMART turns anxiously to PRINCESS INGRID.)
SMART. Okay, he's gone, Princess. You can
drop the pose.
PRINCESS. I don't know what you're talking about.
99. I think it would take a pretty big shock.
SMART (whispering). Any chance of getting loose?
99. Not the slightest.
PRINCESS (gesturing with gun). Don't even try.
99 (softly). *She's* our only chance.
SMART (doubtfully). That possibility sure wasn't
worrying Mr. Big. (The sound of a motor start-
ing up is heard from off R.)
99. If we could find some way to shock her back to
her senses!
PRINCESS. Don't talk so much.
99. I think our time's running out!
SMART (gently). Say there--guard. (PRINCESS
INGRID turns and looks at him and with all his
strength he shouts:) *Smorgasbord!*
PRINCESS (unimpressed). What's that?
SMART (urgently). Scandinavia! Stockholm!
Oslo! Copenhagen!
PRINCESS (shrugging). Shanghai! Nanking! Peking!
Formosa!
99. We can't have much longer!
SMART. Think about snow, glaciers, pine trees,
skiing down a mountain, ice skating!
PRINCESS. What about it?
SMART. Doesn't it stir memories? A young girl
growing up in the north country--stories about
Vikings--Eric, the Red--the midnight sun!
99 (hushed). Keep at it!
SMART. Northern lights--fiords--canned sardines.
PRINCESS. I'm from Hong Kong.
SMART (with all his force). You're *not* from Hong
Kong. You're a Scandinavian princess. Once I

saved your father, and now you can save all of
us! Princess--Scandinavia is in danger! The
whole world's in danger! We've only a few minutes left to stop that madman!

PRINCESS (putting gun on table, straining to com-
prehend). I don't understand--it's so confus-
ing----

SMART. Princess! (Expels a breath.) What's
the use? I just can't reach her.

99 (eagerly). But you are! You're beginning!

PRINCESS (straining harder). Certain words--
words you were saying----

SMART. Hopeless. I simply don't understand
these new methods--brainwashing--hypnotism.
(Bitterly.) I guess I belong with the other an-
tiques in the Smithsonian Institute.

PRINCESS (pouncing). *Smithsonian Institute!*

99 (carefully). What about it?

PRINCESS. Why do we have to go there?

SMART (a little indignant in spite of himself).
What's *wrong* with the Smithsonian?

PRINCESS. Really, Max!

99 (exultant). *Max!* (Turning to SMART.) You
broke through! (The sound of motors comes up
again.)

SMART. We'll take you *anywhere*, Princess. But
there's one thing we have to do first.

PRINCESS. What's that?

SMART. Save humanity.

BLACKOUT

(The action continues without pause, moving rapidly in the darkness.)

PRINCESS. What happened to the lights?

99. Quick--we're tied to the chairs--cut us loose!

SMART. Come on! Use your dagger--hurry!
   (Doors slam offstage during this and there is
   the sound of someone running. At the same
   time an engine is being revved up.)
99 (released and rising). Why would they switch
   off the electricity?
SMART. Something's gone wrong! (Also released.)
   Thank you, Princess.
99. We need reinforcements, and we need them fast!
SMART. There's no time. We're on our own!
PRINCESS (delighted). This is really exciting! I
   love it!
SMART. Love what?
PRINCESS. What you said--saving humanity.

(A MAN runs onstage UR carrying something and
   shouting.)

MAN. Never! Never! I won't allow it! *Never!*
   (SMART has out a flashlight which he turns on
   the man.)
SMART. *Professor Dante!* (DANTE is revealed,
   clutching the scale model of the Inthermo.)
DANTE (heroic). You *can't* use the Inthermo to blow
   up the Statue of Liberty!
SMART. *We* don't want to blow up the Statue of
   Liberty! We're on *her* side! (Another door slams,
   and more running is heard.)
DANTE (frantic). The *other* side--they'll be on us
   in a second! What can we do?
SMART. Deactivate the Inthermo. We'll try to
   cover you.
DANTE. Deactivate--right! (Quickly placing machine on table.) I need light. I blew out the house
   current just before I made my dash.
99 (using her flashlight). Here----(Voices are heard
   shouting from off R.)

VOICES. He didn't come this way! Block the other
    door!
DANTE (at machine). Now, let's see--circuit B
    deflects the coils--or is it circuit C?

(GARTH rushes on U R with a flashlight, which he
    turns on SMART.)

GARTH (with grim pleasure). At last! My favor-
    ite dream--eliminating Maxwell Smart!
SMART (turning his flashlight on GARTH and mov-
    ing toward him in a judo posture). Well, I al-
    ways respect a man with ambition.
99 (to DANTE). You've got to hurry!
DANTE (working). Now--if I reverse the central
    induction unit--I can discharge the current and
    get an *awful* shock--so I don't do that--wait----
    (SMART and GARTH are apparently having a
    titanic battle in the darkness, their flashlights
    waving in every direction, with grunts and the
    sounds of blows coming from each of them.
    Voices are heard again, shouting from off R.)

VOICES. He's got the Inthermo! Get it back--we
    have to shove off! Move!

(Someone--MARY WONG--darts on stage.)

99 (calling anxiously). We've intruders, Princess!
    (There's a brief commotion.)
PRINCESS (as she struggles). I've got one!
99. Hold on.
DANTE. Wait a minute--this should be simple.
    Now--if Farmer Brown takes five molecules to
    the market--and Farmer Green takes three----
PRINCESS (urgently). Watch out! Here comes
    more of them!

SMART. Turn out your lights and make a run for
it. (The flashlights are snapping off.)
GARTH. Oh, no, you don't!
SMART (grabbing flashlight from GARTH). Oh, yes,
I do! (He turns that light out, too, and in the
darkness there is the confused sound of people
rushing this way and that, followed by a moment
of silence. Then the sound of the engine comes
up very loud and continues for an instant. This
is intended to represent the sound coming from
Mr. Big's speedboat. It begins to diminish apparently as the speedboat is driven off into the
distance.)

(After the sound fades out, the light comes up on the
L side of the stage, revealing CONTROL head-
quarters. The CHIEF stands behind his desk.
HODGKINS stands back behind him. MISS FINCH
waits at the side of the desk, with 99 near her.
SMART, PRINCESS INGRID and PROFESSOR
DANTE are on the right side of the apparent
room.)

SMART (taking a breath). Chief, it was dark--and
they managed to escape in their speedboat.
CHIEF. *With* the Inthermo.
SMART. The speedboat was moored in the river
right next to their base of operations in that restaurant.
CHIEF. We should stop that speedboat before it
gets out of the Potomac! It's a long way to the
Statue of Liberty, but at the speed they'll be
traveling----
HODGKINS (looking off U R). I can see a lot of
activity out there on the water, Chief.
SMART. Right. I radioed the Coast Guard and
they're full speed with everything they've got on

a collision course with Mr. Big!

CHIEF (desperate). Max--what happens to the
  Coast Guard, when Mr. Big uses the Inthermo?

SMART. To the Coast Guard? Nothing!

DANTE (surprised). What?

SMART. Listen to this, Chief--listen, carefully.
  (Speaking with great clarity.) Mr. Big is about
  to destroy himself!

CHIEF. How?

SMART. Professor Dante switched the controls!

CHIEF. Switched the----

DANTE (shaking his head violently). No, I----

SMART (clasping his hand over Dante's mouth).
  It's beautiful, Chief. Wait till I tell you!

CHIEF (startled). Max, have you lost your----

MISS FINCH (putting in). There's something very
  peculiar about----(But she is stopped when 99
  grabs her in an apparent judo hold, putting her
  hand over her mouth, too.)

CHIEF (dumfounded). What are you----

SMART (a frantic gesture with his free hand). Listen! (Crossing toward desk, bringing DANTE
  with him.) Listen to how Mr. Big will destroy
  himself.

CHIEF (holding himself in for the moment). Okay--
  we're listening.

SMART. When Professor Dante got to the machine,
  he switched controls--he switched "activate"
  with "self-destruct"! (PROFESSOR DANTE
  shakes his head violently, but SMART holds his
  hand tightly over his mouth. 99 also has to hold
  MISS FINCH tightly for she's struggling, too.)

HODGKINS (has taken out binoculars and is looking
  U R). Looks like Coast Guard cutters closing in
  on the speedboat!

CHIEF. Go ahead, Smart! What happens?

SMART. Don't you see----(Leaning toward MISS
  FINCH and speaking carefully.) When Mr. Big

pushes the "activate" button, he's really pushing "self-destruct." He'll blow himself up!

(Immediately, on this, the VOICE of Mr. Big, as heard over the loudspeaker before, comes on. They all look up, frozen.)

VOICE. Hello, CONTROL. This is KAOS. CONTROL, this is KAOS. Our compliments again to Mr. Smart. We are receiving you loud and clear, Mr. Smart. We have the Inthermo lined up on the Coast Guard cutters and I hope you'll enjoy the display. You said too much about your little switch, Mr. Smart. (Triumphantly.) Instead of pressing "activate"--thanks to you--I will now press--"self destruct"! (There is a blast from the loudspeaker, and then silence.)

HODGKINS (gripping binoculars). *Wow!*

CHIEF (bitterly). The Coast Guard cutters destroyed? Thanks to Smart?

HODGKINS. No--the KAOS speedboat!

99 (still holding MISS FINCH). Thanks to Smart.

DANTE (free now and indignant). I did *not* switch the controls.

SMART. No, Professor Dante, but Mr. Big *thought* you switched them.

DANTE (realizing). I see.

HODGKINS (still with binoculars). Look at that boat burn! It's a blazing inferno!

DANTE (clasping hand to his head). *That's* what I meant to call it--Dante's inferno!

CHIEF (still uncertain). Max--how could you be so certain Mr. Big would receive you?

SMART. Because I located their bug.

MISS FINCH (to 99). Let go of me.

CHIEF. Where?

99. Here. (Indicating bit of jewelry worn by MISS FINCH.) This little pin shaped like a spider.

CHIEF. *That's* the bug?

MISS FINCH (protesting). Costume jewelry.

99. A highly sophisticated transceiver.

SMART. Remember when she walked back into the
room again, and my little detector came on a-
gain? I took one look at her pin, and I knew--
that's the bug!

CHIEF (to MISS FINCH). Shame on you. (Turns.)
Hodgkins, take her out and book her.

HODGKINS (taking her arm and starting her off L).
I'm supposed to advise you of your rights. You
can make phone calls, hire lawyers, have a jury
trial, appeal the verdict----(They have completed their exit L.)

PRINCESS. You showed me an exciting time, Max.
(Frankly.) But I'm about ready to go home. For
one thing, I want to help my father get ready to
hold the NATO meeting.

CHIEF. Wonderful!

PRINCESS. And for another--I seem to be incredibly homesick. I don't know why, but suddenly
I'm longing for Northern lights--fiords--canned
sardines.

DANTE. If it wasn't for Mr. Smart, maybe none of
us would be going home.

99. Max did such a wonderful job, Chief, maybe you
should let him give the good news to the President.

CHIEF. That's a good idea, 99. (To SMART.) Better call him right away.

SMART (giving 99's arm a squeeze as he passes her,
touched). Thank you, 99.

99 (softly). You deserve it.

CHIEF (as SMART reaches across desk, sharply).
No, Max----(Forcing himself to speak pleasantly.)
Not the red one.

SMART. Of course. (Taking off his shoe.) I'd rather use this one anyway--for sentimental reasons.

(Glances at red telephone for number as he dials shoe. Apparently his call is answered and he stands at attention.) Sir--this is Maxwell Smart of CONTROL. I am happy to report our mission is accomplished. Princess Ingrid is safe. The NATO meeting will proceed. Professor Dante rescued. KAOS destroyed. And I take great pride in saying that the forces of darkness have once more been foiled in their attempt to extinguish the bright torch of liberty! (The curtain starts falling. SMART pauses, then continues into shoe.) What? The wrong number--sorry. (With a determined expression on his face, SMART starts re-dialing.)

THE CURTAIN FALLS

PROPERTIES

GENERAL: Central office of CONTROL: Well-equipped desk with intercom and two telephones, one red and one white; file cabinets, several chairs, large hanging map of world with markers stuck in it. On desk: Papers, file folders, small box of fish food, several photographs of blonde girls, ash tray. Hotel room: Several chairs, small table with telephone on it. Mr. Big's room: Screen, four chairs, table with telephone on it. Restaurant: Two or three small tables with chairs, small gong, high stool. In front of curtain: Three lockers, numbered 13, 14, 15. Trash can.

HAND PROPERTIES, Act One:

HELEN and MYRA: Small table with odd little mechanism (the Inthermo) on it.
JANE and FRED: Stand with curtains around base.
FRED: The "target," a small container holding concealed flash bulbs.
SMART: Handkerchief, trench coat and hat, slip of paper in pocket of trench coat, revolver, notebook and pencil; locker key.
ZALINKA: Clipboard.
CHIEF: Pipe.
HODGKINS: Small case containing key, fountain pen, cuff links and cigarette lighter.
MAN: Suitcase, small portable radio.
GARTH: Newspaper; four sets of earphones.
BIG SISTER: Suitcase, newspaper.
LITTLE SISTER: Suitcase.
AGENT 13: Blackjack.
HELEN, MYRA, JANE and FRED: Trash.
AGENT 44: Telephone.

SHIRLEY WONG: Large gaudy poster (ad for Fortune Cookie Club) and tacks or tape.
BETSY WONG: Small bowl containing fortune cookies, leaflet, book matches and ash tray.
MR. BIG: Small metal device.

HAND PROPERTIES, Act Two:

HELEN, MYRA, JANE and FRED: Notebooks and
trash.
ZALINKA: Trash.
AGENT 99: Telephone, wrist watch, flashlight.
SMART: Fortune cookie, small object (description
on page 62), wrist watch, flashlight.
PRINCESS: Arms container, gun.
BETSY WONG: Menus.
DANTE: The Inthermo.
GARTH: Flashlight.
HODGKINS: Binoculars.

CHART OF STAGE POSITIONS

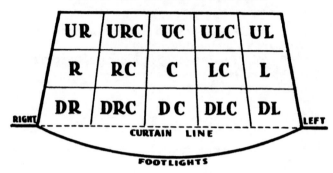

STAGE POSITIONS

Upstage means away from the footlights, *down-stage* means toward the footlights, and *right* and *left* are used with reference to the actor as he faces the audience. R means *right*, L means *left*, U means *up*, D means *down*, C means *center*, and these abbreviations are used in combination, as: U R for *up right*, R C for *right center*, D L C for *down left center*, etc. A territory designated on the stage refers to a general area, rather than to a given point.

NOTE: Before starting rehearsals, chalk off your stage or rehearsal space as indicated above in the *Chart of Stage Positions*. Then teach your actors the meanings and positions of these fundamental terms of stage movement by having them walk from one position to another until they are familiar with them. The use of these abbreviated terms in directing the play saves time, speeds up rehearsals, and reduces the amount of explanation the director has to give to his actors.

WHAT PEOPLE ARE SAYING about *Get Smart*...

"My students did not grow up with Maxwell Smart, but through the magic of "Nick at Night," they were able to revisit Control headquarters. Actors and audience alike loved the shoe phone and trash can scenes. *Get Smart* was a big hit."
Pam Lyng, Hannibal Middle School, Hannibal, Mo.

"A delightful comedy that incorporates all the characters, clichés and gadgets that we loved from the television series."
Lucas Matney, Dream Chasers, North Wilkesboro, N.C.

"An hysterical spoof on 'Mission Impossible' and James Bond akin to 'Pink Panther,' but with more recognizable humor and heart. Easy to stage, fun to rehearse and entertaining to watch!"
Teresa Fisher, Grundy Center High School,
Grundy Center, Iowa

"In twenty years of doing shows, I don't know when we've had more fun. Actors loved it; students and parents thought it was hilarious. Thanks!" *Kathleen Ryan,*
Northridge High School, Layton, Utah

"It went very well. The dialogue was crisp and funny. The acting was excellent. What a great show!" *Michael Altmann,*
Edison Intermediate School, Westfield, N.J.